Graham Hart has taught geography both in England and Jamaica, and has held senior editorial positions in various publishing companies. He has contributed articles to *The Times* and *The Times Educational Supplement* and is the author of several books on sport. Now a freelance writer, Graham Hart runs an editorial agency from his home near Cambridge where he lives with his wife and their two children.

GRAHAM HART

THE
FIRST-TIME
FATHER

CORGI BOOKS

THE FIRST-TIME FATHER
A CORGI BOOK 0 552 99320 4

First publication in Great Britain

PRINTING HISTORY
Corgi edition published 1989

This book is set in 10/11 pt Garamond by
Goodfellow & Egan Ltd, Cambridge

Corgi Books are published by Transworld Publishers Ltd.,
61–63 Uxbridge Road, Ealing, London W5 5SA, in Australia by
Transworld Publishers (Australia) Pty. Ltd., 15–23 Helles
Avenue, Moorebank, NSW 2170, and in New Zealand by
Transworld Publishers (N.Z.) Ltd., Cnr. Moselle and
Waipareira Avenues, Henderson, Auckland.

Made and printed in Great Britain by
The Guernsey Press Co. Ltd.,
Guernsey, Channel Islands

Very special thanks are offered to all those fathers who gave up their time to talk about their experiences.

Thanks are also due to a number of others for their help in writing and producing this book: Averil Ashfield, Moira Banks, Chris Forster, Sally Gaminara, Judith and Tom Hardy, Peter Osborne, Alison Paris and Mary Tucker.

The book wouldn't have been possible at all without the guidance of Anne, John and Josie, the trio to whom it is dedicated.

Thank you.

CONTENTS

THE
FIRST-TIME
FATHER

INTRODUCTION

THE ROLE OF THE FATHER

What kind of role can a father expect to play in the birth and upbringing of his child? With modern medical knowledge it would be possible for the father to absent himself from the proceedings entirely – even including the conception! In reality, many fathers today want to be involved as fully as possible in all the various aspects of pregnancy, birth and child-rearing. It is commonplace to see fathers in the delivery room; most can change nappies, mix up a feed and bath and change their children, although this is not to claim that most fathers necessarily *want* to do these things. It is just much easier in today's society to take an active and involved interest in what was formerly 'women's work'.

Giving early thought to the kind of role you may wish to play can be valuable. For the mother-to-be there are certain inevitabilities, but for the father-to-be there is a lot of choice. Just how the father decides to respond to the birth and upbringing of his child can have important implications for both the child and the mother, but finding the necessary guidance to help make an informed decision can be difficult. Most books on pregnancy, childbirth and child-rearing are, not surprisingly, written with the mother in mind. Unfortunately, many of these books relegate the father to the role of disinterested onlooker. The only advice for the father comes under such headings as 'How father can help' or, even worse, 'Can father help?'

This book is for fathers who want to share in the upbringing of their children – and for fathers who aren't sure what they want, but know they're going to have to be involved anyway. It's a book written not by doctors, psychologists or other medical experts, but by fathers themselves. Most of the information is derived from scores of interviews held with fathers.

The book is divided into three sections. The first is concerned with pregnancy and the birth itself, the second with the early months of a child's life and the third with topics of longer-term interest that might deserve some consideration at an early stage.

Apart from the information and reference chapters, each section is in the form of questions and answers. These are questions that new fathers frequently ask, and the responses that experienced (but not necessarily 'expert') fathers provide. This approach gives a realistic and practical approach to the much-debated problem of how to care for and bring up children. The boxed sections are for quick reference. They are not exhaustive descriptions of the subjects in question but tips and hints supplied by fathers. And while all those fathers interviewed were happy to give advice and say what worked for them, they all agreed there could be no right or wrong way to do things. The only feature of having children that was constant for everyone was that life was never the same again.

If you are soon to become a father, or if you have just had a child, the author hopes this book will be helpful to you and wishes you all the very best. As one father so aptly expressed it: 'Whether or not you find the experience enjoyable and rewarding, don't forget that your children are only on loan to you; you must try to make the most of every moment.'

1

PREGNANCY AND CHILDBIRTH

A CHANCE FOR SHARING

It's very hard to talk about the announcement of a pregnancy without using a number of clichés. Pregnancy and childbirth are an 'everyday miracle', the actual birth of the baby may prove to be 'the most wonderful day of your life' and, no matter what fears or worries you have, it will be difficult not to think in terms of the forthcoming birth as a 'happy event'. With the good wishes that normally follow the announcement, and with all the other matters to be considered, one aspect of the whole affair that sometimes gets overlooked is the impact a pregnancy and birth can have on the relationship between the mother and father.

A CHANGE FOR THE GOOD

From what fathers say there is no doubt that the parents' relationship is affected by the events, the good news being that the impact is, more frequently than not, beneficial.

The feeling of truly sharing something is very important. One particular father, while not blaming the pattern of modern society, certainly suggests that his 'eighties' lifestyle had affected the relationship between him and his wife – and that the announcement of a pregnancy brought about a most welcome change.

❝ Nicky and I had lived together for two years before we discovered she was pregnant. Like many things in our lives, perhaps like our unmarried status, it was the result of indecisiveness rather than positive decision-making. So when she said she might be pregnant we were not particularly excited, but certainly not disappointed either. We waited for another few weeks before Nicky said she was going to take a test. During these weeks Nicky said that her breasts were tingling and she felt a little bit off-colour on a couple of mornings; I put these feelings down to her imagination.

I can remember the day of the test very well. It had to be done in the morning for some reason, and so Nicky got up really early, fetched me a cup of tea in bed, and went off to the bathroom. She came back about half an hour later holding a little glass bottle and asking if the shape I could see at the bottom of the bottle was a circle or not. It was perfectly round. We were going to have a baby! Of course, we needed to have a further test at the doctor's a few days later, but from that moment there was no doubt in our minds that Nicky was pregnant and we were going to be parents.

The effect on us was both dramatic and delightful. Almost immediately there was something in our lives (over and above the foetus) that hadn't been there before. It's no exaggeration to say it was like starting all over again. There was excitement in everything we did; we took ourselves out for candlelit dinners and found ourselves together in bed much more than ever before. We got married within two months with Nicky, much to her delight, barely showing her bump at all.

Although we both acknowledged that we had become much closer we didn't like to analyse the reason for the change. We simply put it down to the pregnancy. Looking back at it now, from the happy position of having three wonderful (most of the time) kids, I think I know why we reacted to the news so positively. It was because it gave us a genuine chance to share something. When we set up home together it was not from scratch; we both brought our own personal trappings into the house. We worked in different types of job and so had little in common there. We liked entertaining, the cinema, reading but we tended to do everything as a couple of individuals rather than as a unit. I'm not saying that it was a bad thing, indeed our relationship seemed to work very well, but that we were compatible, convenient, sometimes competitive, but never thoroughly integrated or unitive.

If we shared an experience we would try to stamp our individual marks on it. For example, we would talk about films we had seen or places we had visited until one or other of us 'won' the right to claim it by describing the deeper significance it held, or by finding it funnier, sadder, better or worse than the partner. With the announcement of the pregnancy, however, there could be none of this. We had to share, and our roles were clearly defined. Nicky was allowed to have morning sickness, I was entitled to worry about the bank balance (Nicky worried a bit too). Nicky was expected to learn how to breathe, relax and push while I had to read up about the support I could give during the birth. The more we got interested in what was going to happen, the more we came together. **"**

Perhaps this idea of truly sharing is the key to the positive benefits that a pregnancy can bring to a relationship. Many of today's fathers are part of, or have been influenced by, the 'me generation'. The main emphasis of life lived in this style is a striving for self-fulfilment, not necessarily selfishly but with one's own self at the centre of things. To parents who have tried this way of life, the warmth that comes from a shared pregnancy and parenthood may come as a most agreeable surprise.

DISCOVERING A NEW RELATIONSHIP

Fathers, generally, are not professional, or even amateur, psychologists. They just try to take the events in their stride, not analysing them but merely enjoying any extra benefits as best they can. For many, though, there was no denying that the knowledge that a baby was on the way brought about a significant and recognizable change in their relationship with their partner.

" Everything went much better; all the problems we had before suddenly seemed to become unimportant. The thing that mattered most was the forthcoming arrival and that was something for the pair of us, not anybody else. It was especially nice some weeks into the pregnancy, once the initial interest from others had died down and before the 'have you had it yet' questions began.

We found we were doing so much more together, both for the baby and for ourselves. We sent each other cards and gifts and started calling each other 'Mum' and 'Dad'. It might sound silly but I have no doubt that being happy is good for one's health, and women in particular want to be in good nick during a pregnancy. My none-too-serious advice, if your marriage is struggling and seems in need of a boost, is to get pregnant! **"**

There is no mistaking the genuine expression of joy from that father although, as can be seen later in the book, not all fathers shared the same happy experiences. Some found it hard to get interested in the pregnancy stage, with consequent implications for their relationship, while others found that togetherness became a factor only after the birth and not before.

STORING UP FOR THE FUTURE

One important reason for trying to get the maximum benefit, in terms of the parents' relationship, out of the pregnancy is that after the birth that same partnership is likely to be put to the test. With sleepless nights, drastic changes to one's social life, worries about the health of the new arrival and any number of other stressful factors, any store of love and goodwill that can be created will be most welcome.

" We relied heavily upon the memories of the days before the birth during the worst moments after it. My wife suffered from post-natal depression, not badly but sufficiently so that she would be really miserable at times. What was worse was she knew that she was being sulky and angry, and knew there was no real reason for it, but she couldn't get herself out of the mood. The only things that seemed to help were reminders of how happy we had been before the birth.

One toy, a teddy bear, always eased the situation. We had bought it when we couldn't really afford it, when Tracey was about five months pregnant. As is often the way with us, we then went on and had lunch out to celebrate and spend even more money. We were so happy that we didn't really care at the time. During our meal we sat the bear on a chair but had to move him when somebody, in all seriousness, asked us if the seat was taken. We cracked up, and ever since have used the incident as a kind of 'our song' to help us when things get a bit tense with the baby.

We're now hoping to have another child and both of us, I know, are looking forward to the happy days of sharing and expectation before the birth. **"**

Buying items like the teddy-bear is a part of the process of planning for the birth. It's often this practical preparation that stimulates the feelings of togetherness and harmony that couples so frequently enjoy before the baby's arrival. And since there are some important shared decisions to be made it is probably a good idea to look for every opportunity to demonstrate one's love and affection for one's partner.

Fathers often find this time useful for learning from their partners about some of the facts of childbirth and child-rearing. You may say that the father doesn't need to learn these things from the mother; he can, and ought to, attend classes and read books. Realistically, though, our modern society still aims most information at the mother and she is more likely to have the greater store of information. In one relationship, and this is probably true of many, the partners found that the sharing time before the birth brought about a subtle and beneficial change in the relationship.

" I can see a clear pattern in the way I behaved during Gayle's pregnancy. At the outset I was a bit stunned; I was unused to having events going on that seemed beyond my control. But I soon got to realize that I could enjoy the congratulations and the jokes that go with being a 'pregnant' father. After this stage I noticed that Gayle was getting all the attention and that she was becoming the dominant partner in all matters to do with the coming birth. I found this hard to take since, in anything important in the household, I had been in charge. When it came to knowing about things such as our finances, house repairs, our insurances and legal affairs and so on, I had always taken the upper hand. But now here was something, and something of great importance, where Gayle was definitely in the driving seat.

It took a little while for me to realize that it would be stealing something from Gayle to try to take charge of the pregnancy. In fact, quite the opposite happened. She drew up lists of what to buy and what we needed to do. She read the books and basically taught me the facts about the birth of babies. I always asked her for information.

I don't think it's overstating the case to say that she became an equal partner in what had been, before the pregnancy, an unequal relationship. And that situation has grown. Since Timothy's birth I have become much more involved with the business of bringing up kids, and Gayle has shared in much more of the household decision-making. Perhaps I should not have needed something as monumental as the birth of a child to make me realize that I was a bit bossy and domineering, but I'm grateful for the change in our relationship that Gayle's pregnancy and Timothy's birth have brought about. **"**

THE SIGNPOSTS OF CHANGE

In very many cases where the fathers had noticed a change for the better in their relationship, they identified actual shared tasks that had brought them closer to their partners. Attending ante-natal classes was one fruitful source of the pleasures of sharing. Parents frequently derived useful information from their classes but, as often as not, found the greatest benefits in sharing the sessions with their partners and swapping stories with other couples in the pub afterwards. Buying items for the baby and decorating a nursery were other little duties which helped to pull couples closer together.

The choice of name for the baby is one task that has to be shared and on which might be spent many hours of togetherness, poring over books and scribbling down lists. In truth, it does seem to be something of a minefield – the perfect subject to spark an argument. If you are a first-time father looking for a baby-oriented job to share with your partner, experience suggests you go out and buy a cot cover rather than talk about baby's name!

The choice of name apart (and, of course, it needn't be a problem), there are many jobs that fathers might like to suggest they do with their partner to encourage the feeling of sharing. Simply talking about things, how you as parents are going to cope, whether you want a boy or a girl and on what day you expect the baby to arrive, will provide happy shared moments. Those few fathers who found they missed out on the potential benefits of the pregnancy stage, either because they were away from home or because they were uninterested in the whole business, do mostly express regret at a lost opportunity. They seem to recognize, albeit a little late, what a difficult time the pregnancy can be for the mother. Apart from the possible physical problems such as sickness, heartburn, sleeplessness and excessive weight gain, mothers are often understandably anxious about what's in store for them. To feel isolated from their partners is an additional burden they certainly don't need.

As has been mentioned before, the opportunity to renew or refresh a relationship because of a pregnancy should be given every encouragement, not least because, after the birth, the strength of that same relationship may be tested quite severely. To look at it from a slightly different angle:

> **“** If I knew then what I know now, I would have cashed all my savings in and gone on a cruise – because, sure as I'm standing here, I'm not going to have the chance again while I've got three kids! **”**

DO I NEED TO ATTEND CLASSES?

This is something that you may have sorted out at an early stage of the pregnancy as part of a shared approach to the events that lie ahead. Quite often, however, the question is raised by the father at a middle or late stage of pregnancy, as the physical signs become more obvious and as some of the implications of what has been entered into become more worrying!

Whether to go is only part of the question; what type of class to attend is also something that needs consideration.

THE OPTIONS

Different types of class are offered by different groups and individuals. In the main you will find that free classes of varying types are offered by the hospital, the midwife or health visitor, GP or health centre, while paid-for classes are provided by the local group of the National Childbirth Trust and, occasionally, by other interested parties.

It is unwise to generalize too much because classes differ greatly. Some like to combine ante- and post-natal care in the one session, some are really only for mothers, while others actively encourage the participation of the father. Probably the best advice is to decide what you want from your lessons and then to check out exactly what is on offer.

What do you want from a class? These are some of the areas that might interest you:

- the development of the unborn child
- the birth itself
- looking after your partner
- assisting in pain relief and management
- baby care

Most classes will offer a general cycle of sessions, covering most of the above. The health of the mother is a topic that may be catered for not only in general information sessions but also in more specific relaxation classes especially for women.

The fact that the classes are cyclic means that it's a good idea to decide early on if you want to attend. This will ensure that you have the opportunity of fitting in the complete course before the birth of your baby.

TO GO OR NOT TO GO?

Whether or not it is worth attending classes depends on you, of course. What do fathers think? A majority of those asked thought it was a good idea – but nowhere near the majority attended!

❝ It wasn't until I went to classes that I started to realize the sort of questions I wanted to ask. There are so many little things that it's useful to know. I had no idea at all about the way a baby was actually born and was very pleased to see a film of a birth at the class run by the hospital. Had I not seen the film and had the chance to ask questions at the time I would have found Kay's birth much more worrying and a lot less enjoyable. **❞**

This father found the information about the actual birth useful – it took away some of the anxiety. That might be the key to the question. Attending classes ought to give you a great deal more confidence about what is going to happen. This confidence will probably grow, not only as a result of receiving information but also from sharing the classes with other fathers in the same position as yourself.

❝ I likened the classes to business conferences; the most valuable work was done in the bar afterwards. About four of us fathers would always stop for a chat at the end of the meeting. At first we were a bit coy about discussing matters but we soon got to asking when each other's baby was due, how our wives were getting on and so on. Naturally we had lots in common and therefore lots to talk about. We sometimes came across questions that we wanted to ask and would appoint a spokesman for the next class. Towards the end we were getting very involved and the questions were becoming extremely technical. The poor health visitor who was running the class had to keep checking things out in her books. **❞**

In becoming more confident about childbirth, you and your partner should be able to relax more. An unruffled and calm attitude on the day of the birth will be very helpful. One particular session that many fathers, especially those who didn't attend a full course of classes appreciated, was the hospital visit. These are sometimes called 'fathers' nights', although they are really for both partners. Most maternity hospitals organize these on a periodic basis. You and your partner are given the opportunity of visiting the wards and the delivery rooms and of talking to hospital nursing staff. It means that on the day you know just what you are doing and exactly what sequence of events to expect.

❝ On our visit to the hospital we were in a group of about six couples. At first it was a bit quiet but once we got into the delivery room things started warming up. It was amazing just how ignorant we all were, asking questions about the equipment in the room and what would happen if . . . The nurses were great and dealt with all our silly questions with a great deal of tolerance and good humour.

It was a really good experience, enjoyable as well as informative. We eventually had a difficult delivery with forceps and I was grateful for the little bits of information I had picked up during the hospital visit. We also made a note of the expected arrival dates of the other parents in the group on that night and made a point of looking out for them when our child was born. 〞

PAIN MANAGEMENT

Labour pains are something you will certainly have heard about. You may be concerned about the effect that they will have on your partner. She, understandably, may be quite worried too!

The whole area is interesting in that, on the one hand there is a lot written and said about how to cope with (and even enjoy) labour, while on the other hand there seems to exist a sort of conspiracy of silence among mothers, who tend not to be too explicit about the nature and severity of the pain of childbirth. If you want to find out more, and especially if you want to know if there's anything you can do to help, then six months before the baby arrives is the time to act.

Classes may be the best place to ask questions about the nature of labour pains and how you can best deal with them as a couple. You should hear unbiased information about the various means of pain relief available to the mother. You will probably be aware of the debate about whether to use certain modern methods of pain relief or whether to go for a more natural birth. Classes are the time to voice your anxieties and to get the facts together to enable you and your partner to come to your decision later.

If you decide that you wish to avoid 'non-natural' means of pain relief then you may choose to attend further lessons on relaxation, breathing and even hypnosis. These will probably occur as offshoots of your regular classes. The best advice is to attend classes and talk to others who have tried certain methods of pain management.

❝ I was determined to be as supportive as I could, trying to share the experience as much as possible. It was the matter of pain and pain relief that seemed to be most important. It seemed unfair to me that my wife should have to suffer all the pain; if there was anything I could do I wanted to know. The problem was that I didn't want to interfere.

For the record, we went to classes on hypnosis. They were really just a form of relaxation I suppose. They certainly helped, but at the very end of labour my wife had a pain-killing injection anyway. It made no difference to us or our baby but we were generally pleased to have drawn on our own resources as much as possible before using science to help us. The important point is that we could not have learnt what we did about pain relief without attending classes. **"**

Most fathers who attended classes on pain management ended up talking about 'we', perhaps indicating that shared attendance and shared involvement do really work. There is no getting away from the fact that the woman has to bear the pain, so any discussion about relief ought to consider her views as paramount. The father is there to help, however, and his support will probably be of great benefit.

The reason for talking about pain relief in this part of the book is that there is often a lot of advice on offer when the subject comes up. If you are seriously interested in looking at alternatives and making an informed decision then class attendance is highly recommended. If you wish to follow a particular technique, and wish to prepare for it, then classes may be your *only* option. More information is also provided on page 67.

NATIONAL CHILDBIRTH TRUST

Outside the range of classes and information available through the National Health Service are those sessions run by the National Childbirth Trust (NCT). It's worth mentioning this group separately, not least because you are bound to hear about them, but also because there are sometimes misunderstandings about their aim.

The first misconception concerns the name. They are the *National* Childbirth Trust and not the *Natural* Childbirth Trust. This confusion sometimes leads parents-to-be to assume that their lessons are only for those who are aiming to have a drug- and technology-free labour and birth. This is not the case, although the NCT classes are likely to encourage parents in this direction.

The general aim of the NCT could be described as simply trying to help parents understand and enjoy the experience of childbirth. The style of particular NCT classes will be determined by the person organizing the sessions and, assuming a reasonable level of democracy, the parents who are attending. In some large towns and cities you may have a choice of NCT classes; in these situations it's worth seeking a personal recommendation. Wherever you go you will find a welcome for fathers with the NCT.

The NCT also takes its role far beyond the preparation for the first baby. Local groups, where mothers and fathers can meet, are popular and many have mixed social sessions where those expecting children meet with those who are already parents.

OTHER SOURCES OF INFORMATION

If you are reading this section then you are probably interested in finding out more about becoming a father – hopefully that's why you're reading the book in the first place. Books can be a good source of information, either as a supplement or a substitute for going to classes.

Most books available are for mothers, but that should not deter you. Fathers occasionally get a mention! Importantly, some contain very useful and interesting information about the mechanics of the whole affair. It might be worthwhile buying one of these for reference. Also, some go into detail about the care and health of babies in the first few years of life. Any professional will be able to suggest a couple of useful titles; your bookshop and library should have plenty on offer. Two excellent general volumes are *The Complete Book of Babycare* edited by Barbara Nash (St Michael/Octopus Books) and *The Reader's Digest Mother and Baby Book* edited by Geoffrey Chamberlain *et al*. For a shorter book you might find the *Pregnancy Book*, given away free by the Health Education Council, to be very useful. Of the few titles specifically for men, the best bet is probably *The Expectant Father* by Betty Parsons (Paperfronts).

❝ We had one book that was a real bible for us. I'm glad I found out as much as I did. The knowledge gained from the book helped me follow the pregnancy with much more interest. **"**

" We had a couple of books that I must confess I only looked at in detail about a month before Jenny was born. I wish I had read them earlier. **"**

DO I WANT TO KNOW THE BABY'S SEX BEFORE THE BIRTH?

HOW IS IT DONE?

The most common method of finding out the sex of a baby, and perhaps the only way likely to be offered to you by medical staff, is simply by looking at the child at the time of a sonar scan. With normal pregnancies the woman will probably have a scan at around eighteen or nineteen weeks. If you want to know your unborn child's sex, this is the time to ask. The operator of the scanning camera may be able to say whether your baby is a boy or not (identifying a girl is simply a matter of being pretty sure that it's not a boy). However, it should be pointed out that this method is not entirely foolproof, and may not even be possible if the baby is curled up in a certain way in the womb. So even if you and your partner decide to ask the medical staff for the news, you can't be completely confident of the right answer or, indeed, any answer.

It should also be pointed out that, in some pregnancies, a test called amniocentesis may be carried out. Most commonly the test is recommended by doctors for older mothers where the risk of Down's syndrome in the baby is slightly higher than for younger mothers; it can also be used where there is reason to suspect diseases such as spina bifida, haemophilia and muscular dystrophy. The process involves extracting a small amount of the amniotic fluid, the fluid surounding the foetus. This will be analysed for tell-tale signs of disease. As a by-product, the analysis will also show up the sex of the baby. This should be a foolproof method of diagnosing the sex. If your partner is asked to undergo amniocentesis, you can ask the sex of the baby. You cannot, however, ask for amniocentesis simply to satisfy your own curiosity.

WHY ASK?

The key question, however, is not *how* to find out but *why* find out. Why spoil such a secret?

“ Like so many fathers I was faced with the possibility of finding out our child's sex before its birth. I wondered why I should break with the tradition of ages. Then I thought: why not? Science has made it possible so perhaps it's just a natural step to take. After all, my wife and I were happy to take advantage of every other opportunity that science presented. We knew we were having just one child, we had a rough idea of its size, we knew approximately when it was coming; why not find out its sex, too?

In the end we decided to keep the suspense up and wait until the birth. It was a boy. And I think that we were pleased we didn't know. It made the moment a bit more special – and a bit more traditional. The midwife who did the delivery actually said, as they do in all the films: "It's a lovely, bouncing, baby boy. Congratulations!" We were happy with our decision. **”**

It seems that only a tiny handful of parents asks to know the sex of their child before its birth. Those that do ask are frequently second- or third-time parents. One of these described his reasons for wishing to know as 'simply financial'. The father in question was keen to decorate a room for his new child – he already had two children – and wanted to get the decor right. This approach might imply a degree of sexual conditioning but, within this context, it demonstrates one practical reason for wanting to know the sex of the unborn child. Did this father find the birth of his child anti-climactic?

> **❝** I liken the experience to flying in a plane. On the first occasion I flew in a modern jet I was terribly excited and enjoyed every minute of it. Thereafter, and with each succeeding flight, I have been more nervous. Perhaps it's because I know what can go wrong or because I feel that soon my number will be up. With children, the first birth is amazing; the second is no less amazing but somehow less overpowering. By the time you get to the third and beyond you're just grateful if your child and wife are healthy. It doesn't get easier. Thus, knowing the sex beforehand was not important; my only anxiety was to get the thing over with.
>
> My advice to new fathers is, don't find out for the first baby – enjoy the whole experience. Thereafter? You're on your own. **❞**

There's no getting away from the fact that it's all down to personal choice. What do you and your partner want? The general view was, wait until the day – don't spoil the magic.

However, the one first-time father interviewed who did find out the sex of his child – because of a slight medical complication with the baby – was not unhappy with the information.

> **❝** I was slightly more concerned about my wife's health but I don't think that knowing beforehand would have caused any problem even if it had been a completely normal pregnancy. In fact we enjoyed knowing, because it became like waiting for someone to come and visit – even though we were expecting them to stay quite a long time! We chose a name, Amy, and kept talking about "once Amy's here" and "that will be after Amy's at home". So when Amy actually arrived we were well prepared. Now, of course, it's like she's never not been here. **❞**

Is it possible that one partner wants to know and the other doesn't? One father told about the 'friend of a friend' whose wife wanted to know but who didn't want to find out himself. For weeks beforehand the wife had to be very careful not to spoil the surprise for the father. In the heat of labour, just minutes before all was to be revealed, she called out: 'typical man – keeping me waiting'. Secrets seem inadvisable, and hard to keep.

IS THE FATHER REALLY WANTED AT THE BIRTH?

IT'S YOUR CHOICE

Assuming you are not hoping for a birth at home, this is one question that you will be faced with long before the actual day. This is not because the hospital will be asking, but because everybody else will be. 'Do you intend to be there?' is one of the commonest questions put to 'pregnant' fathers. Pete had the answer before his big day.

> **“** It's no good me even thinking about going because I would faint. Once I saw the blood and the doctors and nurses with all that equipment I would be a heap on the floor – and more trouble than good. I'll be happy to wait outside puffing on cigarettes and pacing up and down. **”**

And that's exactly what Pete did (although he wasn't allowed to smoke in the hospital). To this day he doesn't feel he missed out on anything because he's convinced that he would have passed out anyway. This may be true, for some people do experience this kind of reaction to the sight of blood. Certainly Pete's point about being more trouble than good is valid if he was sure to faint. Many fathers are a little squeamish, but most of them seem to cope.

> 66 I was not sure about how I was going to react to the medical side of things. I wasn't looking forward to the use of surgical implements; and that smell of hospitals is enough to make me feel weak at the knees anyway.
>
> But when I was there I was so swept up in events that I didn't have a moment to think about it. Just watching the skill of the nurses, trying to follow all that was going on and generally attempting to be helpful but unobtrusive took all my attention. And when Victoria was actually born it was so fantastic that I wanted to cry, not faint.
>
> Of course I should say that I was pleased to be there to support Liz, but she was so groggy with the injection and with tiredness that somehow I ended up spending more time at the bottom end of the bed than the top! 99

HELPING YOUR PARTNER

The last father's mention of his partner is a useful reminder that the decision about whether to be present at the birth is most likely to be a shared one. Perhaps the most important aspect is the support that the father can give to the mother. Mothers are squeamish too, of course, and many may be seriously frightened of the likely pain, the possible medical problems, and just the actual moment of birth itself. Your partner may not like to relay these fears to you before the day, although once labour has passed its very early stages, she will probably be less reticent about these anxieties! So from this point of view attendance at the birth is something that fathers do for their partners as much as for themselves. But this doesn't mean that they won't get anything out of the experience.

Labour may last many hours and, depending upon the policy and situation of the hospital, there may be long periods in either the ward or delivery room when there is no member of the medical staff in attendance. These are good moments to enjoy and, the mother's labour pains permitting, to talk about baby's likely sex, name, birth weight, and even the weather.

❝ We had shared the pregnancy quite a lot. I went to classes with my wife, we read lots of the books available and I was always doing things like feeling the baby when it kicked. But the time of the birth was the best. It pulled us together so much, not only the moment when Penny eventually emerged into the world but also the hours before. We had shared things previously like holidays, our wedding, our first home and so on, but nothing quite like the sharing moment of birth. The woman does all the hard work, of course, but it's still something that you, as a couple, have made together. **❞**

❝ Basically it was magic. I cried when Mark was born. It took hours to get there and that probably accounted for my emotional state. But you can't beat it. I took some photos and got the nurse to take one of the three of us. It's a poor photograph but I think it's the one I treasure more than any other. And if you're asking me what other fathers should do, that's easy – be there. **❞**

The fathers who were present at their child's birth all agreed it was an event not not be missed. Most enjoyed the whole thing, particularly the closeness of it all; some found it the most moving event of their lives, and a few actually enjoyed it for the medical interest. It is important, if you plan to attend the birth, to check that this is acceptable to the hospital. They will tell you what you are allowed to do. Not all hospitals will agree but you do have a moral, if not a legal right to be present. Persevere if objections are raised.

With home births the situation is very different. The various health authorities have differing policies on this. From your point of view the decision to have your child born at home probably means you have already also decided to be present at the birth.

Because of the sense of togetherness, the excitement of the birth itself and the support that you can give your partner, it is highly probable that you are going to want to be present at the birth. Indeed, aside from your partner's feelings, it might be hard to resist the outside pressures on you to attend. However, do remember that it's very unlikely that your own father was present at your birth, and that not all fathers feel they have something to offer. Does this make them poorer fathers?

> ❝ It's a woman's job. The woman bears and produces the child and throughout history it has been the role of women – family, neighbours, midwives – to be present at the birth. It's only just a phase, perhaps a reaction to women's lib, that means that men are expected to be there. I missed the birth of both of our children and they haven't suffered one bit because of it. ❞

So it's up to you. Dozens more quotes could be reproduced from fathers who did attend, each describing how special the moment was. Above all, though, the fathers described the birth as an intensely personal moment, and to experience it you've got to be there, in person.

HOW MUCH IS IT GOING TO COST?

A CAUSE OF ANXIETY

The best advice might be to think about the cost of having a baby before your partner becomes pregnant. However, the truth of the situation is that, although the cost is often considered, it is rarely the determining factor in a couple's decision to start a family. It is only once the woman discovers that she is pregnant that the financial implications start to trouble the parents. By this time, of course, it's too late to do much about the arrival of the baby, but some idea of the cost might help in planning. Simply to know that other parents have coped is a great comfort. The last thing you want to be doing during a pregnancy is worrying about money; this will spoil what can be a very special time, and may cause your partner great stress at a period in her life when she's got plenty of other things to think about.

Shock stories about the birth and first year costing £10,000 and the total bill from birth to eighteen years being £100,000 are complete nonsense. You *could* spend this amount if you tried hard, and if you had the money, but you would probably be very foolish to do so.

    ❝ We had agonized over whether to have a baby for some time.
       Cost was always the main point of my argument, while Beth

would come up with emotional reasons to support her point of view. You can guess that she was in favour of having a child; I was against it.

I used to add up our total income and then start subtracting. The first item to come off was Beth's salary. This was followed by the cost of baby equipment and the extra food and heating that we would need having two people at home all day. No matter how I did my sums I used to come up with a hopeless position. Assuming no repairs to the car and nothing increasing in price in the meantime, it would appear that we would have about £11 per week for all extras, e.g. clothing, entertainment, anything other than household essentials, newspapers, etc. We knew that we were lucky both to have jobs and to own a house, but for a couple used to having, and apparently *needing*, about ten times this amount my calculations were cause for considerable despondency. And then Beth got pregnant!

So we were faced with this desperate prospect of moving from a life of relative comfort to one where we would be struggling to buy even a pair of shoes for ourselves. We both thought we could manage but worried that we would become very depressed and unhappy and eventually would end up by resenting the presence of our baby.

The fact that I can talk about, even joke about it, now is simple proof that things did not turn out as badly as I had expected them to. I forgot about at least three things in my calculations. The first was the child allowance of about £7 per week; this was quite useful and used to buy the nappies. The second was the generosity of family and friends. We received so many gifts of both hand-me-downs and even new items that we hardly needed to buy a single item of clothing, or, for that matter, anything much at all. And the third was that we had no idea how much the arrival of a baby affects your lifestyle. Beth had given up smoking the minute she knew she was pregnant and stayed off ciggies right through Julie's first year. I found I was cutting down on many of the times when I was having a pint or two, just so I could be at home with the family. And naturally we didn't go out nearly as much together at first. A really good night for us was sitting up in bed, watching television and feeding and nursing the baby. **"**

GETTING BY

Interestingly it's the fathers-to-be who try to work out the exact costs. Once a child has arrived, both partners seem to have too much else on their minds to count out what's actually being spent.

> 66 Having kids isn't easy – at least, not in our experience. But the one thing that didn't seem to bother us was a lack of money. We were very hard up but never admitted that it had anything to do with the baby. We'd blame lack of sleep, lack of social life and general tiredness for our arguments and unhappiness ... but we'd never mention money. Chrissie went back to work soon after Jodie was six months old, and that helped a lot, but even so it was a very difficult time. However, as I said before, we never really argued about money. 99

This father didn't analyse the reasons why he and his partner kept money out of their arguments. Was it because that would have been an admission of taking a wrong decision or, perhaps, because they knew there was a danger of 'blaming' a four- or five-month-old baby for their problems?

The father in question may well have looked into the financial situation very carefully and emerged as one of the 'we'll get by' school of thought. This particular method of accounting seems very prevalent among fathers who have just looked at the costings and don't like what they see. Although it would be irresponsible to give any support to this approach, it does seem to work. Many fathers said that they simply didn't know how they were going to get by and yet, in the end, they did. Perhaps it should also be recorded that fathers pointed out that the first two or three years were not, in fact, the problem; the big expenditure came when the children started school.

The reason for this ability to 'get by' when the estimates all look pretty bleak may have a lot to do with the changed lifestyle that parents experience after the birth of their first child. Much is said, in this book and elsewhere, about how life will never be the same again. This is certainly true financially, but it's not all bad news. These are typical comments.

"" For six months we hardly went out at all, and we didn't mind at all. Plenty of people came to see us, and we would often have friends over for tea on a Sunday. But we found that we didn't go out for meals or to the cinema as we had done before. Most noticeably we didn't just pop out for a quick drink – we couldn't. Cutting out those unplanned visits to the pub must have saved us ten to fifteen pounds a week. Had I been asked beforehand I'm sure I would have reacted strongly to this loss of freedom. In the event, I couldn't have cared less. **""**

"" We found we were spending more time with friends who had children of their own and that often they were in the same financial situation as ourselves. If we wanted to have a meal together we would share the cooking and exist on home brew. There was no embarrassment. Relatives and friends recognized the situation we were in and made allowances, although I have to say we didn't really go short of anything. It just always looked as if disaster was around the corner. **""**

"" We were hard up, but actually not as badly as we thought we were going to be. And as baby Alan had to come first we had no qualms about refusing invitations or not buying presents because it was obvious to us, and to anybody else I guess, that we had to cut our cloth according to our means – and our means had changed after the birth of Alan. **""**

Many more examples could be quoted of how fathers feared the worst, and yet ended up being both surprised and relieved about the realities of the financial situation. But although there are many fathers who cheerfully accept life on a much tighter budget, there is no denying that the whole affair can be made more comfortable if there's a bit of spare cash around. If you've got some savings, or if you've got a good salary that isn't all needed, then you are going to have less to worry about. If this is the case, pages 43–52 give you some ideas about what you can spend your money on.

This section is supposed to answer the question 'how much?', and so far no realistic figures have been mentioned. The reason for this omission is, by now, probably clear. There is no way of putting a price on it – and if you try you'll probably be agreeably proven wrong.

Perhaps all that can be said is that it may well prove cheaper than you expect, that the savings often come from unexpected quarters, and that you'll almost certainly have plenty to take your mind off any money worries once the baby arrives. If you can count on savings, so much the better, but assuming that you're already an expectant father, use the period before the birth for other things rather than constantly poring over depressing calculations. The message is: you'll probably get by.

WHAT SHOULD WE PROVIDE BEFORE THE BABY ARRIVES?

The previous section in this book deals with the total cost of having a baby. It comes to the conclusion that you can't put a price on it. You buy what you can afford, and what you think you need, and then hope for the best. This section looks at the sorts of things that might enter into your calculations in planning for your first child – a few necessities and a few luxuries.

MATTERS BEYOND YOUR CONTROL

Your decisions about what to provide for the new baby will probably be made jointly, so the advice is not specifically for the father. However, in many households it is the father who is given the role of managing the family budget and so some idea of what others have experienced may be useful. Furthermore, it's not practical to try to prepare a list of what should and should not be purchased; there are so many different opinions. But it is possible to look at the general problems associated with providing for a baby and to hear what some fathers particularly recommend.

❝ My wife and I are not mean but, like a lot of people, we've been brought up to be careful about money. In the months before Nathaniel was born we were reminded of the build-up to our wedding. The expense seemed to grow and grow. There didn't seem to be any control over it. It wasn't only what we were buying but what other people, mostly relations, gave us. We ended up with much too much. We were both unhappy about it; I suppose we felt a bit guilty really. We had more things than we needed, which made us feel uneasy, and we had things we didn't want or need but which we felt we had to use in order to show gratitude. **"**

The comparison between a birth and a wedding is a valid one in many respects, not least in the matter of spending money. The birth, like the wedding, is a time of traditional happiness and gift-giving – therefore it's a time of opportunity for the manufacturers and retailers of babycare products. It would be very easy to criticize these groups for creating unreasonable demand through their advertising, but a more practical response is to be grateful for the range of goods available and to try to decide exactly what is needed.

GETTING BACK TO BASICS

A new baby is like any other human in that it needs food, clothing and shelter. One important difference, however, is that a baby is not as mobile as an adult and therefore needs some means of being pushed or carried around. Looking at these basic needs is probably the best way to plan the arrival of the baby. Once the basics are covered, the rest can be seen as useful (or not so useful) extras.

FEEDING THE BABY

The food element is something that, initially, will be determined by whether or not your partner decides to breast-feed. While breast-feeding, the expenditure on food will be for nourishing meals for the woman, rather than the baby, but there are a few ideas worth considering.

“ We were very keen that Joe should be breast-fed, and happily Ros was able to do it. Apart from any nutritional and emotional considerations, it was simple and efficient. This was especially true when we were out, providing our hosts didn't feel bothered by it. Breast-feeding, however, can be both tiring for the mother and unrewarding for the father.

So, before Joe was born, we bought some equipment for storing a mother's milk and for giving it to the baby with the aid of a bottle. This was useful on a number of counts, not least because it helped in weaning Joe, something that can be quite tricky. ”

If breast-feeding is rejected as an option, or if it is not possible, then some provision for milk must be made before the baby's arrival home. This is an essential, and is simply a matter of personal selection from the many types available. Advice will be given at the hospital and/or by the midwife. It must be remembered, though, that the milk and bottles are not enough and that sterilizing equipment is also needed.

---

bottle-feeding essentials

- six bottles with teats
- sterilizing equipment
- bottle brush
- supply of baby milk
- small saucepan or use of microwave oven

Even if your partner is going to breast-feed you will need a couple of bottles with the related sterilizing tackle for the times when baby may require water.

“ We were lucky in having parents who had given some money to their first grandchild, my niece, and decided to give us the same for our child. We felt that we had to buy something special and not spend the money on a variety of items. We eventually bought a microwave oven which, at first, seemed a little selfish but actually proved to be the best hundred pounds we had ever spent.

Because we didn't decide on the microwave for a couple of weeks after the birth we knew what life was like both before and after. Initially we would prepare a drink for Lynford by placing one of his bottles in a pan of water and warming it in that way. Inevitably we would overheat it and then spend minutes running it under a tap while Lynford cried. The microwave meant we could get the exact temperature in about one-fifth of the time. This was especially important at about three in the morning.

Our final conversion to the microwave was when we were told that it could be used for sterilizing bottles and other

---

first clothes: the bare essentials

- nappies – 24 terry nappies or supply of disposables
- vests – 4
- stretch suits (babygrows) – 4 (or 2 suits and 2 nighties)
- bootees – 1 pair
- mittens – 2 pairs (scratch mittens may be useful for the nights)
- cardigans – 2
- hat (sun hat or warm hat depending on time of year) – 1
- shawl – 1
- pram suit – 1

The list above is of essentials, but you won't actually need a great deal more because baby will grow out of things very quickly indeed.

baby equipment. We were able to dispense with a very cumbersome sterilizing kit. Had we known, we would not have bought it in the first place but gone for the microwave from the outset.

I suppose it goes without saying that Lynford's parents also enjoy some of the benefits of the microwave! **"**

CLOTHING THE BABY

Clothing is the area where gifts are most commonly given. These may include second-hand clothes from other recent parents or lovingly knitted shawls and jackets from relations.

---

what to consider when buying clothes

· make sure the clothes are easy to put on and take off – poppers are better than buttons and the more of them there are the better
· be sensible in choosing fibres – natural are usually much better than synthetic
· babies grow quickly, so buy large
· your baby knows nothing about fashion, but a lot about comfort

---

" We were given so much it was quite embarrassing. Most of the clothes were from parents who had recently had babies. The clothes came with the warning, 'we'll have them back when we have another'.

We gratefully accepted them all but realized that our child would never be able to wear everything. When you think about it you can see why there are so many clothes for young babies around. The children grow so quickly that the clothes never get a chance to wear out.

About three or four weeks before the baby was due we sorted out all the various items of clothing and realized we probably had enough of everything. This saved us money but, in a curious way, we felt that we had missed out on something. So we went out and bought one outfit, in the style we liked, for a couple of quid. Daniel wore this when he came home from hospital. I was happy to have actually chosen something – although generally I found it easy for the father to be left out of all discussions about baby clothing.

Apart from the homecoming we were not fussy and dressed Daniel in anything we liked. Having said that, we did try to avoid offence and tried to remember who had given, or lent, certain things so we could dress Daniel in the right outfit when he visited the relevant uncle, grandmother or friend. **"**

" I found that I was not involved much in building up the wardrobe for Melanie. It didn't really interest me; I had wanted a daughter and was fairly keen to see her dressed in frills and bows – but knew my wife's taste was better than mine so left it to her.

But asked for advice I would say one thing: get clothes that are easy to put on and take off. Fathers who take an active part in bringing up the baby will realize very quickly just how important this is. A good friend of mine is a gardener and his hands are very large and very hard. Seeing him struggle with tiny buttons on the back of a woollen top is quite touching. Poppers and zips are best and even, if it's obtainable, Velcro.

The one-piece jumpsuits, commonly called babygrows, are ideal. Don't worry about appearance, worry about comfort and practicality! **"**

The fathers talking above have, by their own admission, been fortunate in receiving gifts of clothing. In situations where presents are not forthcoming and where the budget is very tight, the warning about comfort and practicality is very apposite. Babies grow very quickly and have no interest in fashion. They want to be comfortable and warm. If you are planning the spending of limited resources these are important points to remember.

While worrying about what clothes to buy or borrow it is possible to forget that all-important item of baby-wear, the dreaded nappy. Unless you are the most enlightened and egalitarian of families, with friends and relations of similar outlook, you will find that most, if not all, conversation about nappies is directed towards your partner. The main talking point concerns whether you're going to use disposable or washable nappies. With only two options available it would appear to be a simple decision.

---

changing baby – what you will need

· if using towelling nappies:
  · waterproof pants – 4
  · nappy pins – 6
  · nappy liners – 1 packet
  · sanitizing powder
  · soaking bucket

· for both towelling and disposables:
  · changing mat
  · cotton wool
  · baby lotion and cream

· optional extras:
  · changing bag – if you expect to go out a lot
  · 'baby wipes' or 'Wet Ones' for cleaning up baby on the move
  · sanitized disposal bags for use with disposable nappies

But, as with buying anything else, you can be sure that somebody will scoff at your decision. If you want to get involved in the debate, the main fighting ground is over cost (for washable) and convenience (for disposables). No matter what manufacturers say, it is cheaper to use washable and easier to use disposables. It proves nothing, but may be of passing interest, to note that most fathers interviewed for this book favoured disposable nappies.

ACCOMMODATION AND MOBILITY

In addition to food and clothing you will want to give some thought to the problem of accommodation and means of mobility for the new arrival. As above, it is preferable to make plans before you bring the baby home.

---

for bath and bed

· plastic bath, tub or bowl
· baby soap or liquid
· soft towels – 3

· cot or crib
· firm mattress (ideally plastic-coated)
· waterproof undersheet
· normal sheets – 4 (minimum)
· blankets, duvet or quilt

❝ Looking back it's funny what silly mistakes you can make. Our major one was to plan the baby's room in the coldest part of the house, pushing our heating bill up considerably.

Another problem arose because I had decided to put the finishing touches to the room while Joan was in hospital. When we eventually had the baby home the smell of paint was so strong we couldn't consider using the new nursery for a week anyway. **"**

Apart from points of commonsense, as above, there's not a lot to worry about with regard to accommodation. You may be surprised by how small your young son or daughter is. Providing a baby has warm bedding, the actual surroundings are largely immaterial – a drawer makes a very successful cot if you're stranded without proper equipment.

The new baby's mobility is important to the parents, whether this is likely to be in a pram, on public transport or in a car. The best advice seems to be to decide how the baby is most likely to be moved and plan accordingly. If the baby is going to be wheeled to the shops every day, and if the major excursions are going to be just around the corner to visit family or friends, then a traditional high-wheeled pram might be ideal. For frequent car journeys a detachable carrycot with pushchair base may be best.

You will receive no end of advice from other parents and from manufacturers and retailers. You will find that there is every combination available, from grand 'carriage' prams to 'lie-back' buggies, suitable for the very young but adaptable for toddlers. A popular choice is the all-in-one affair where a carrycot on wheels can later be adapted to become a buggy-style pushchair. Additionally, when thinking about mobility, don't forget the options offered by slings and pouches – normally front slings for the very young and rucksack style for slightly older children. Overall the choice is difficult, all the more so because of the expenditure. However, if you have a clear and unromanticized view of your life-style, you should be able to make the best decision.

For the sake of economy do remember that many prams and cots are multiple use, and that your baby will not stay one month old and weighing eight pounds forever.

Today, car seats are available for the very youngest babies. These are mostly of the type which fit on to the front passenger seat and which are held in place by the seat belt. The baby faces the back of the seat. Their main disadvantage is that mother or father get to sit in the back of the car! The only other option, as mentioned above, is to have a carrycot that can be strapped on to the back seat.

ANYTHING FOR YOURSELF?

Fathers have little excuse for giving themselves treats during the pregnancy stage; it is going to be your partner who needs maternity clothes, special bras and a variety of other accoutrements. One or two suggestions for useful items, apart from the more facetious ones such as 'a bottle of Scotch', 'a win on the pools' and 'a mistress', are worth noting.

> **"** The best thing we did was to begin renting a video machine about six weeks before Mark was born. We either went to bed early because we were tired and watched hired films, or else we watched our favourite soaps at three in the morning whilst feeding the baby. Whatever it cost, we more than saved the money by not going out so much. **"**

> **"** I bought a diary and, for the first time in my life, found I kept it. Nothing much, just a few entries about Dawn's progress and, occasionally, something about myself. If we have another baby I'll do the same, although I might possibly use a hand-held dictation machine instead of a diary. **"**

> **"** We bought a video camera and relive, very frequently, some of the magic moments when Christine first got home from hospital with Peter. An expensive toy, but worth it. **"**

> **"** I bought the most interesting-looking book I could find about pregnancy and childbirth. Whenever Avril wanted to chat about the pregnancy I could hold up my side of the conversation. We actually argued about some points, her book's views against those in my book, but overall it was a very useful purchase for us both. **"**

WHAT ABOUT SEX DURING PREGNANCY?

THE COMMONSENSE APPROACH

This is another of the questions about fathers' experiences where it is difficult to generalize. For every father consulted there was a different story to tell.

From a medical standpoint there is no risk to baby or mother during the period of normal pregnancy providing, of course, that the woman is as careful during her love-making as she is during the rest of the day. Women who experience any vaginal bleeding during pregnancy, or during love-making, will be well advised, however, to visit their doctor. As the pregnancy develops your partner will probably find that she is becoming increasingly sensitive and she will probably express the wish to make love very gently. Whether her feelings are based on physical sensitivity or a psychological desire to protect her baby is immaterial – the request is obviously important. If this sensitivity becomes acute then a visit to the GP is probably wise, although his or her advice is likely to be unsurprising – to stop love-making until matters improve or the baby is born. A commonsense approach is clearly what's needed.

Commonsense should also be applied to the matter of *how* you make love. Towards the end of the pregnancy your partner will almost certainly find it difficult to move in the same way as before.

The most popular and comfortable position for couples during this time is usually the female back to the male front, 'like spoons'.

One theory that you may hear is that love-making can bring about the start of labour. This is certainly one piece of advice offered to couples whose baby is late in arriving. It is possible that there is some truth in it, either because the physical movement sets the chain of events in motion or because a hormone secreted during sexual intercourse acts as a trigger. Again, providing you take all the care due to your partner, there's no danger to mother or baby in love-making right up until the last minutes before the onset of labour.

A MATTER OF ATTITUDE

Interestingly, it was not the physical side of sexual relations that caused the most problems or comments. It was the emotional response to love-making, and in particular the woman's attitude to her body, that was cited as causing the greatest number of changes to a couple's normal pattern of behaviour.

“ My wife used to say that she felt "fat and horrible". There was no point in protesting that she didn't or that it was a natural process and she should enjoy it. She felt bad about her appearance and there was nothing much I could do about it. This fact certainly curtailed our love-making. But, to be quite frank, it didn't really matter much to us anyway. We knew that things would return to normal and so had the best part of a year, eight months before and about three afterwards, where we hardly had sex at all. **”**

“ Dorothy was not very happy about her body, or about me seeing it. We had a very open and honest relationship so I was a bit surprised to see her covering herself up more in the bedroom. I really didn't mind what she looked like.
As a result of Dorothy's attitude we made love a little less often during the pregnancy. I also don't think that Dorothy enjoyed it as much. It was all to do with her size and how she saw herself; I don't think it ever hurt or was uncomfortable. **”**

It is reasonable to assume that some men might have a similar response to their uncontrollable growth if they were the ones carrying the babies. The second of the two mothers mentioned above was a very keen volleyball player, a sport she had to give up for the duration and to which she has not returned since the birth of her child. For somebody who enjoys using their body for recreational purposes, a pregnancy might be quite unsettling for this reason alone.

In some cases, fathers-to-be found that their own feelings changed.

> **❝** I know that my wife was unhappy about her body and her weight during the pregnancy. I didn't like it much either. I know I was supposed to enjoy her new "natural" shape, but I much preferred her when she was slim and weighed eight stone. That sounds awful – I didn't "prefer" her then but I was certainly more "aroused" by her. Whether my feelings were too obvious (of course I didn't say anything at the time) I don't know, but we made love less often during the pregnancy. We didn't stop, however, and we derived as much pleasure from it when she was pregnant as ever before. **❞**

And finally, this father-to-be, in the minority but still representative, was able to paint a quite different picture of sex during pregnancy.

> **❝** Right at the end we were really careful and gentle. Until then, however, there was not much difference. If anything, we did it more often. Of course, we had to make certain positional changes! But no, I can honestly say that the pregnancy had no detrimental effects at all. I thought my wife looked really lovely. Her breasts were beautiful, although sometimes a little tender towards the end of the pregnancy. We would often lie still after making love to see if we had woken the baby up. I'm looking forward to the next pregnancy, although, what with Toby waking up once or twice in the night, it might be a bit different this time around. **❞**

HOW WILL MY PARTNER'S HEALTH BE AFFECTED?

There was recently a famous family-planning poster that showed a man in the late stages of pregnancy; he had a large, distended belly, and the warning implied that men would be more careful about contraception if they were the ones that ended up in this condition. There is something that tends to upset many men about a loss of control over the body. With an illness you can try to fight off the symptoms; with a pregnancy you largely have to welcome the changes and make the most of them. Men should, perhaps, be grateful for the biological reality of life (although how long will it be before a foetus can be implanted into a male?) and simply do their best for their partners in the months of pregnancy.

A GENERAL APPROACH

How best to help your partner may well be determined by her approach to the pregnancy. Being pregnant is a natural state and one that has probably been entered into happily and intentionally. If this is how the partners feel then the changes in a woman's body, and all the possible problems associated with them, can be seen as necessary and even interesting developments. If pregnancy is seen as an abnormal state or an illness then the changes, and certainly the problems, may be resented.

But problems, although fairly common, should not be uppermost in your mind when the pregnancy is first announced.

> **"** We had always hoped to share the whole experience and so were naturally keen to do the best we could, collectively, when Andrea found out she was pregnant. The first thing to tackle was my smoking. Andrea had given up smoking some two years before, but I had never managed to kick the habit altogether. When I smoked, just occasionally, at home Andrea would say how much she wanted to have a cigarette too. I always used to say "why don't you?" Now she was pregnant there could be no question of her smoking and so I decided to quit immediately.
>
> I'm sure the first weeks of the pregnancy were worse for me than for her. Oddly enough, it made me feel I was contributing something. Later in the pregnancy Andrea had many sleepless nights, partly as a result of heartburn and partly from being unable to find a comfortable position in which to lie. This also gave me an opportunity to get involved, as I would sit up with her and talk or watch videos. I also used to be the one to go downstairs to get the milk, which is supposed to help heartburn. **"**

The couple above tackled the man's smoking. Having a healthy and balanced diet is as important as not smoking and represents another area where co-operation not only helps the woman in practical terms but encourages a feeling of sharing the experience of pregnancy. Drinking alcohol, needless to say, is a further area where the woman needs to be careful and where a partner can be supportive.

PROBLEMS FOR THE WOMAN

Unfortunately, no matter how well a pregnancy goes the mother-to-be is likely to suffer some problems. These range from common and irritating complaints such as morning sickness and backache to the more serious difficulties of high blood pressure and vaginal bleeding.

It is a very good idea for the father-to-be to read through the list of possible problems that any proper medical guide will contain. By doing this he will be able to reassure his partner that what she is experiencing is quite to be expected or, in serious cases, will be able to take the decision to call on expert advice. If you know that your partner has a tendency to hypochondria, then you would probably be wise not to discuss any of the problems until such time as they actually appear – if, indeed, they do.

There is a commonly held belief that many of the problems of pregnancy are induced by negative emotions such as anger, anxiety or fear. This is not to say that a woman who suffers from varicose veins is not looking forward to her child's birth, but that sometimes the body responds badly to the extra pressure, both physical and emotional, that is placed upon it. There is no evidence to suggest that a woman with the most positive attitude imaginable cannot suffer from the full range of problems; similarly, a bitter and unhappy mother-to-be can experience a completely trouble-free time. What is suggested is that there is a greater likelihood of an easy pregnancy when the mother-to-be is relaxed and confident. It is only sensible for the man to try everything possible to encourage this state of affairs.

But if problems do occur there is not much more to say than 'be supportive'. Commonsense will tell you, for example, that a woman who is excessively tired needs extra help and extra sleep, and that a gentle stroking of the back can ease pain and tension. It will also be commonsense that tells you when you ought to seek medical advice for a problem that has gone beyond what the books describe as normal.

BLOOMING, NESTING AND CRAVING

This small section is included for no other reason than that fathers-to-be seem to have heard about these things and always ask about them. Perhaps it's because these are aspects of pregnancy where something over and above the normal ways of nature appears to be at work.

'Blooming' describes the state of radiant good health that pregnant women are often lucky enough to enjoy, commonly in the middle part of the nine months. That a woman blooms is often accredited to the fact that the body, during pregnancy, is working very efficiently and that the woman is probably enjoying a healthier diet and more restful lifestyle than normal. This seems to be borne out by the fact that first-time mothers bloom more commonly than do mothers with other children to look after. Coupled to these biological elements is the fact that normally friends and relations are hoping to be able to say how well a woman looks – it's simply much more fun, and much more supportive, than saying how tired or unwell she appears. Finally, it's most likely that the woman looking forward to her child will bloom more readily than one who isn't. So, while there's nothing too mystical about women blooming, it's something to be encouraged and enjoyed but not something that you've got to do, or something over which the father-to-be has much control.

'Nesting' or 'nest-building' describes the common occurrence towards the later stages of a pregnancy when the woman will go to seemingly excessive lengths to tidy up the house, clean the nursery, lay out and check all the baby's clothes and perform any number of household chores.

> **‹‹** We used to joke about nest-building but it became a rather serious matter some four or five weeks before Debbie was born. Linda had tended to be responsible for the housework and had always kept the place clean and tidy. I, too, was a fairly tidy person so there had never been any arguments about the way things were in our house. Then, almost overnight, we entered a strict regime of tidiness and cleanliness. Small jobs, like beating out a couple of the mats or wiping down the tiles round the hearth, ceased to be weekly tasks and became daily chores instead. And if I was ever to leave anything lying about it was hurriedly picked up and I was severely admonished.
>
> At first we argued about things but we quickly realized just what was happening. I tried to co-operate as best I could, even down to some silly things like cleaning the radio casing and scrubbing a wicker log basket, and we generally joked a little more about the whole thing. Linda knew she was doing it – but couldn't stop herself. The whole period only lasted a couple of weeks; we soon had other things to think about. **››**

The basis for nesting is fairly obvious, but why it affects some women to such a degree is not quite clear. Understanding that it is as common and as normal as, say, morning sickness, helps to put it into perspective. As opposed to morning sickness, though, nesting is generally not unpleasant and the father-to-be can get involved in supporting his partner in a positive way.

It's easy to see also how a woman's 'craving' for a particular type of food or drink can be biologically linked to her body's need for certain minerals or vitamins. But when you come across mothers-to-be who have found the need to sniff mothballs or chew on pieces of coal, the connection is not so obvious. The fact is that many pregnant women do have strong desires to eat, sniff and even feel certain substances. Providing there is no harm in the action, then the best advice is probably again to be supportive and try to appreciate that some things in pregnancy don't really need an explanation.

More likely than a craving is the opposite situation, where pregnant women suddenly find they don't like foods or drinks they have enjoyed all their lives. This dislike is often linked to things that, in excess, might be harmful anyway. Coffee and alcohol are two common examples.

At the risk of sounding repetitive, the best advice in all these aspects of pregnancy is to support your partner and use common-sense. You can't go too far wrong with this approach.

WHAT ABOUT NATURAL CHILDBIRTH?

In recent years there has been a lot of talk about 'natural childbirth'. One might be forgiven for believing that a simple choice is on offer: natural or 'unnatural'. One might also be led into thinking that natural childbirth is somehow associated with being a vegetarian or belonging to certain Eastern religious groupings.

There should be no mystery about natural childbirth. The whole process of pregnancy and birth is as close to nature as you can get, a fact that will be brought home forcefully to you should you be present in the delivery room. Natural childbirth, in basic terms, is the experience of pregnancy, labour and birth without the use of drugs. Choosing natural childbirth does not mean you are opting to have your baby under water or squatting behind a tree; you and your partner can enjoy a natural childbirth quite happily and legitimately in a sterilized hospital delivery room.

WHOSE DECISION IS IT?

Before looking a little more closely at what factors fathers found important in their decision-making, the question of whose decision it is needs consideration.

The experience of pregnancy and childbirth is something that belongs to the woman, and the hours of the actual labour and birth are the most intense and special feature of that experience. How much a woman wants to share the experience depends largely upon the type of relationship that she enjoys with her partner. Elsewhere in this book the question of whether the father wants to be present at the birth is raised. But what of the case where the woman does not want her partner there? Does she have the right to ban him from the birth of his child? There is no doubt that the hospital would agree to the mother's demands in such a case. So is the situation the same when it comes to deciding how a child should come into this world?

** ** There seemed to be no doubt in our minds that we would go for a natural birth. We are both very opposed to the use of drugs in our everyday life so it seemed only natural that we should follow this philosophy through into the pregnancy. We were also a bit frightened of the possible consequences of a wrongly administered anaesthetic.

About one month before the birth, and a good way through our National Childbirth Trust classes, Sheila met an old friend who talked about her experiences in labour. She was very explicit and quite serious. At first this surprised us, because most mothers tend to laugh off the pains of labour, or not even talk about them – at least, not with mothers-to-be. But this woman weighed in very heavily, so much so that Sheila began talking about the drugs and other non-natural techniques she might use if things got bad. We had always had the idea, in the back of our minds, that we would resort to drugs and modern medical techniques if it really became a matter of life and death. Following our talks with Sheila's friend, however, we were discussing pain-killers and spinal-block injections as if they were inevitable.

I reacted strongly to this at first, saying, rather foolishly, that Sheila was throwing overboard all we had planned and putting the baby's life at risk into the bargain. It was when I got most strident that the question was asked: who's having this baby, you or me? That set me thinking. It was our baby but, at the crucial moment, I was hardly a key member of the team! I felt I had to concede. Although I was unhappy I realized that, in the few exciting yet tense weeks leading up to the birth, the last thing we wanted to be doing was arguing about how to have the baby.

Ultimately it was a fairly difficult labour and Sheila benefited from the use of pain-killers at an early stage of proceedings. At the time I was so overcome with the birth that I didn't care how it had been produced. Subsequently I have felt a sense of disappointment. I think it could have been a much more moving event had we gone through the whole process of labour without drugs. I know from Sheila's comments that we are heading for an argument should I raise the issue again if we have a second child. **"**

One interesting point is the way the father talks about 'we' in the experience of labour. It is not unreasonable to expect that most mothers, while accepting that men can play a role, will say that labour is a uniquely personal experience, and one that men can really know little about.

The attitudes of the parents in the case described above can be reversed, with the father urging the use of drugs. This next father, knowing his comments were being used for research for a book, made some interesting opening remarks.

" I know I'm completely out of line with modern thinking, and that all the other fathers you'll talk to will disagree with me, but I think that natural childbirth is a fad, like not eating salt or jogging. [Many fathers agreed with his assessment – some had even stronger views!] If modern science can ensure a safe birth, without pain, then why bother learning how to struggle on without pain relief? You don't have your appendix out while controlling your breathing to ease the pain, so why go through the agonies of birth?

Needless to say, Elizabeth disagreed with me. She went to classes to learn about natural childbirth and determined to try to go through the whole business without pain relief. I wanted her to have a very quick birth, on the floor of the taxi like in the films, so that she wouldn't be put through any prolonged pain. I did respect her views but secretly expected that she would have to give in. This sounds like a battle, so I could say "told you so", but it wasn't really like that. In the end Elizabeth had a long labour, the nursing staff used all sorts of injections and drips, and the baby was delivered happily and safely.

We haven't talked about our disagreements since the birth. At the time, Elizabeth was not in a really fit state to decide what she wanted, and I didn't object much when pain-killers were suggested. I feel a little bit guilty, but I'm pleased that I've got a healthy wife and child – and so don't really care. **"**

One might answer the question we started out with by saying that the method of birth is ultimately the decision of the mother. But as has been hinted at above, in the heat of the moment the mother may be so emotionally and physically drained that she might welcome some support in her decision-making. It is in these moments that a common and caring approach, developed over a long period of thought and preparation, might benefit both partners. But can you prepare for something when you don't know what to expect?

THE NATURAL EXPERIENCE

The main reason for couples choosing natural childbirth is not a negative aversion to drugs but a positive desire to allow the woman to experience the pain – and more importantly the pleasure – of the intense natural processes that childbirth entails. It's probably true to say, although this may be an over-generalization, that the modern movement for natural childbirth is a reaction to the medical advances made in the past twenty to thirty years. The advances in question could, and sometimes did, reduce the pregnant woman to the status of a problem – how best to get the child out, with the minimum of fuss and bother. An over-zealous, but probably quite well-intentioned, use of anaesthetics could leave the woman with little or no feeling in her body at the climactic moments of the birth.

" We made a positive decision to go for natural childbirth. We were encouraged by our doctor, who gave lessons on how to use methods of hypnosis during the labour, and by the teachers at the NCT [National Childbirth Trust] classes we attended. Of course, the implication of our decision had the greater effect on my wife; after all, she was going to have to try to control her pain while I could only look on and help a little, with the methods we had been taught.

On the day, we got through to the last half-hour or so of labour. By this time Ann was getting very tired and very strained. The nurse, who knew our desire for a natural birth, suggested that a little pethidine might help to relax Ann and help her retain her strength. In a quiet moment between contractions Ann and I quickly discussed it and agreed that it would be a good idea. I say that we 'discussed' it but it was really Ann's decision. I knew she wanted me to agree to her wishes, which I did without any qualms. By this stage we were getting very excited about the arrival, but also a bit anxious. It seemed to be taking such a long time.

Anyway, she had the injection, which is supposed to take about twenty minutes to work, and within the half-hour had produced the baby. Natural childbirth notwithstanding, it was the most wonderful moment of my life. **"**

This kind of experience is fairly typical – but what happened afterwards is, hopefully, not. The same father:

" Ann and I had taken so much from the NCT classes that we thought we'd go back to some of the sessions to talk about our experiences. We felt that we had a very positive and happy story to tell. Much to our surprise, certain members of the new class looked upon us as having failed at the last hurdle. Their views, I have to say, were not discouraged by the teacher.

Ann and I don't feel any sense of failure, but others may do so if they set their minds too determinedly in one direction. We felt we had a natural birth, despite the injections. That may seem a contradiction, but it's one we can live with. Most important of all to us is the fact that the baby is safe and well. **"**

Mothers will be told, time and time again, that nothing can properly prepare them for the experience of childbirth. There is a lot of truth in this, so is it sensible to be too dogmatic in what you want to happen?

WHERE TO HAVE YOUR BABY

Much of the discussion to date has assumed that you can choose the type of birth you want and that the hospital staff or the midwife will heartily agree and that's the end of the matter. Not true. The situation varies greatly, and the part of the country in which you are having your baby is an important factor.

If you decide you want to proceed with a natural childbirth, or even if you wish to proceed as far as you can without drugs, then it is a good idea to discuss your views with those who will be involved with the delivery. This may be the midwife, your GP or staff at the hospital. If you get an unsympathetic hearing then ask a different member of the medical profession or explain your problem to the local branch of the National Childbirth Trust.

> **❝** We knew that the hospital would consider themselves to be bending over backwards just to allow me in at all. Any talk about "natural" childbirth would be seen as mumbo jumbo. We decided to proceed with the birth at the hospital and try to dissuade the staff on the day from administering any drugs. Some of our friends had made a big issue out of the situation and, we felt, had alienated themselves from the staff. We took the soft option with the intention of trying to minimize stress and upset at such a difficult time.
>
> On the day we had a fairly ordinary delivery. Franny had an injection and also some gas and air, but we never felt we were losing control of events. It could have been better, probably, but we've no complaints. **❞**

For couples with stronger views than those expressed above, the hospital situation described would have been intolerable. In these situations alternative places of birth might be considered. The normal options are:

- at home, with the midwife or GP assisting the delivery
- in the hospital, but with your 'personal' midwife involved (this is sometimes called the DOMINO method)
- in a private hospital, sympathetic to your wishes

- in a special maternity home or area health centre which offers maternity care, often under the supervision of your own GP

The only advice that can be offered is to keep asking and to choose what you, as a couple, want to do. You may find help in surprising quarters.

> **"** We had never talked about "natural" childbirth because it wasn't something that our friends or relations had ever discussed. We had always lived a fairly natural sort of life, close to animals, and, in our ignorance I suppose, never thought that there were so many drugs and things. It was only a couple of days before the birth that somebody asked if we were going to "have drugs" or go for a natural birth. We had no idea!
>
> In the hospital we had a wonderful midwife who led us step by step through the labour. My wife was in considerable pain but never thought to ask for pain relief. The midwife never really mentioned it. Right near the end she slapped a mask over Penny's face for a few moments – and that was that. John arrived!
>
> Looking back, we are very grateful for the midwife's sensible and sympathetic approach. Some friends have laughed at our experience, saying "ignorance is bliss". I suppose they're right. **"**

Although the father in question didn't express it in so many words, he and his partner experienced a 'natural' birth not because of a deeply felt philosophy but because it was the obvious thing to do.

HOSPITALS AND PAIN RELIEF

Throughout this section, and elsewhere in the book, we have mentioned various methods of pain relief. The reason why these attract so much attention is that there is considerable discussion both about their respective merits and about their overall suitability for use in childbirth.

The four methods listed in the glossary are those which are the most likely to be offered to your partner (although some others do exist). They are as follows:

gas-and-air   analgesics (most likely pethidine)
TENS   epidural anaesthesia

Since you are likely to hear about them from members of the medical profession, your wife and from friends and family, it is worthwhile to understand both how they work and their respective pros and cons; it's also interesting to hear how some fathers feel about the particular methods.

Apart from the information provided here it is a good idea, however, to read up more fully about what is on offer or to attend classes to discover for yourself. The hospital visit is a good time to look at the various machines and implements that may be used. You can make a decision about the birth of your child only if you have a sufficient supply of information to help you.

Gas-and-air or *inhalation analgesia* is normally used as a self-administered method of pain relief. It involves simply the use of a mask supplying a mixture of nitrous oxide and oxygen (thus 'gas and air' is not an accurate description) which can be held over the woman's face; once the technique has been explained to you it can be easily used without further supervision. You can be of great assistance in its application, particularly during the later stages of labour, by holding the mask, advising when to inhale and when to rest and trying to time contractions; this last point is because gas-and-air is most helpful if used moments before a contraction really gets going.

On the plus side, gas-and-air is reckoned to provide a very effective method of relief. Unfortunately the use of this method has to be restricted to moderately short periods of time, especially during the later stages of labour, because over-use can create breathing problems in the mother. It also produces a slight sensation of drunkenness or light-headedness, effects which may be undesirable. Generally, however, the method is very safe and can cause no ill-effects at all to the baby.

    ❝ My wife, although accepting that she might not care at the time of labour, was not very well disposed to the use of needles. We had the impression that it was an injection or nothing. We had heard of using gas, but we thought it was something like laughing gas, and that it would make the woman temporarily unconscious, a bit like the old stuff they used to use in the dentist.

It was the midwife who suggested gas-and-air and it worked very well for us. I felt involved; in actual fact I felt like a doctor! It had no ill-effects at all and, apart from a bit of drowsiness, my wife felt fit and well throughout. It was only a short labour, about two hours, but the use of the mask made it a lot less unpleasant than we had been led to believe it might be. **"**

Of the *analgesics*, the most commonly used is pethidine. It is a simple pain-killing drug that is administered mostly in the early stages of labour. Analgesics like pethidine may be used in conjunction with a mild sedative because it's thought wise to allow the woman some pain-free rest to prepare herself for the later struggles.

The reason for giving pethidine only in the early stages of labour is that the drug passes through the placenta and can slow down the onset of the baby's breathing, an obviously undesirable effect nearer the time of birth. Apart from that drawback, pethidine is safe and effective.

" Because there is so much light-hearted banter about how much labour hurts and how men never experience anything like it, I tended to lose sight of the enormity of the task that Corinne faced. We did discuss the use of pain-killers before the event but knew in ourselves that we would take the advice of the medical staff on the day. In retrospect that approach worked although, of course, I've no way of knowing how different things might have been had we tried to get through without the use of drugs.

By the time Roddy was born, and following both pethidine and gas-and-air, Corinne was like an old dish rag – pretty wrung out. Her recovery afterwards took a long time too; I suspect it would have taken considerably less time if she had gone through the labour without the injections. She was also sick quite a lot during the labour, something that was probably a direct result of the pain-killers. Ultimately, however, our baby was absolutely fine; for Corinne and me, that was the bottom line. **"**

TENS is the abbreviated form of *trans-electronic nerve stimulation* – a form of self-administered pain relief which acts by triggering off the body's own response to pain before the natural defences, the endomorphs, would otherwise be stimulated into action. Left to their own devices, they would often be too late for the peak of each contraction. The TENS kicks them off early, so they're buzzing away efficiently when the contraction is at a maximum.

In practice the woman has electrode pads attached to the key areas at the base of her back; these are wired up to a hand-held trigger. At the vital moment, just before a contraction is due, she can 'fire' the stimulators which bring the endomorphs into action.

This method is totally safe; the equipment is driven by a battery about the size of those used in small calculators and neither injections nor drugs are involved. The only drawback is the lack of effectiveness if used over a period of time or if the pain has become quite severe. TENS is ideal for the early and middle stages of a short labour.

Epidural anaesthesia is a method of pain relief which enables the woman to remain fully conscious but unaware of the sensation below the position of the needle. Local anaesthetic is piped into the part of the spine through a catheter; the catheter is left in place so that the dose can be topped up if necessary. The whole procedure requires a considerable degree of skill from the anaesthetist and, during the intial injection and installation of the tube, the strictest care with regard to hygiene has to be observed.

Epidurals are often used for Caesarean section or if labour is likely to be very long; there may be some unpleasant side effects when the drug wears off and, occasionally, it may not be altogether effective.

Despite this last point the epidural is probably the most completely effective method of pain relief. Those critics of the method point to the woman's loss of sensation in the vital birth-effecting areas; the drug may so numb feelings that the woman may have to be told when she is experiencing contractions and when she has to push. This increases the chance of a forceps delivery and may take away some of the very sensations that the woman was looking forward to having.

The epidural is sometimes called the epidural block. This should not be confused with either the less well known pudendal block (injections around the vagina) or the rarely used spinal block anaesthetic (a once-only injection into the spine).

66 We heard a lot about the pros and cons of using an epidural. For some of our friends it was the saviour. For others the word "epidural" was akin to the word "leper". Fortunately the medical staff put the whole thing in perspective by their matter-of-fact approach.

You're in pain, you can have pain relief. If you do, the chances are you will lose some of the pain, and some of the associated joy of relief, that goes with a natural birth. The choice is yours.

The fact is that no amount of discussion beforehand can actually prepare you for what is going to happen. This is not only because of the intense nature of the experience, but also because no two labours are alike. For me to go on about whether to plan beforehand, and what steps we recommend for pain relief, would be to make me guilty of something I criticize in others. It's got to be a personal decision. All I would say is: don't be too rigid; leave room for changing your mind when the going gets rough! 99

This father's views echoed the majority both in his advice to be flexible and in his received opinion on the use of an epidural. Apart from the way in which the drugs used deaden the experience, there is also some concern felt about injecting a drug so close to the spine.

66 That was quite frightening. The whole procedure demanded such obvious skill from the anaesthetist that I found myself holding my breath and offering a quiet prayer while he inserted the various tubes. I know that there's very little risk, but you can't help feeling anxious when you've got your wife and almost-born child lying out in front of you. 99

To this problem the only solution is to discuss the risks with the doctor, ideally some time in advance of the day.

As mentioned earlier, the whole area of pain relief, not surprisingly, generates a lot of interest. In order to bring an end to this particular discussion it's worth recording the views of two fathers; their comments were typical:

> **"** Don't underestimate the pain that labour produces. I know my wife very well and just how tough she can be. In short, it must have hurt. I'm glad I didn't have to go through it – and I won't joke about it again either. **"**

> **"** Whatever you choose beforehand, don't rely on that being your final decision. There's a lot of difference between how you feel when chatting over coffee one evening – and how you'll think at three in the morning, in a delivery room, when waves of pain are sweeping over your wife and she's screaming for help. **"**

WILL PATERNAL FEELINGS GROW?

WHAT ARE PATERNAL FEELINGS?

New fathers and fathers-to-be frequently worry about whether they are feeling paternal. Giving advice to others or trying to work out your own situation is very difficult because the term 'paternal feelings' is hard to define. Of course, there is no true answer. The emotions are almost impossible to describe, although one father did explain that he found the situation the same as being 'in love': 'You can't really describe it but you tend to know if you've got it!'

There often seems to be a sort of guilt complex about not having paternal feelings. Just before the birth fathers-to-be worry that they are not mentally prepared for the arrival, and for a while after the birth many fathers feel that they have not experienced the emotional upheaval they were expecting. For want of a better description, these supposed psychological shortcomings may be explained as 'not having paternal feelings'.

But are they important, and should we try to experience them? If fathers themselves believe they need to feel paternal, then importance should be attached to the question.

❝ The announcement of Mary's pregnancy was a big event in itself. We both came from families with no young children so we were announcing the beginning of a new generation. Everybody was delighted and we received almost daily congratulations from friends and family. This period lasted about three or four weeks, by which time most people knew about us and simply looked forward to the actual birth. Our lives seemed to slip back into a very regular pattern. We still went out in the evenings, work carried on as normal, we went on holiday; everything was as it always had been.

It was then I began to worry about my response to the whole thing. I felt no different at all. Mary was busily involved in attending clinics, reading books and getting a mountain of advice from other women. I could accept this as being only natural, but I worried that I had no feelings towards our unborn child whatsoever. I realized that Mary would feel differently because the baby was actually growing inside her, but I wanted to experience a change as well.

It is very hard to explain what I wanted to experience, but I knew that I was expecting some emotional change. In an attempt to start the process I began taking an interest in Mary's lump. I would put my head on Mary's stomach at night and talk to it! The conversations – monologues actually – would be pretty meaningless, but I enjoyed them. Just as talking to the trees, the speaker tends to benefit more than the listener. Perhaps talking to the unborn baby was all tied up with redefining the relationship with Mary. I don't know. But it made me feel good and I will do it again if we have another child. **”**

This father didn't say whether these chats with his unborn child (son, as it turned out) gave him the missing paternal feelings. But they were fun for him, and probably for his partner too. In the later stages of pre-natal development the child can hear in the womb, so allowing it to hear dad's voice can do no harm at all.

PRACTICAL STEPS TO HELP

Attempting to develop a relationship with the unborn child is a practical way of solving the problem – if, indeed, one perceives it as a problem.

> **❝** People always told me I was very undemonstrative, and also not very good with children. I just thought I was typically English! But because people occasionally expressed surprise that I was about to become a father I began to worry about my response to the event and, in particular, to our unborn child. You could say that I was anxious about my ability to be paternal. Would I love the child enough? Was I feeling right? Was I like other expectant fathers?
>
> I did the only thing I felt possible. I took steps to ensure everything was right for the baby. I decorated the nursery, made lists of things that we ought to buy, built a wooden toy-box and bought some toys to go in it. So, although I can't claim that I experienced any great personality change, at least I felt ready for the arrival and knew I could welcome my son or daughter into the home.
>
> Everything since our daughter's birth has proved to me the old adage – that your life will not be the same again. People now say I'm soppy, and I love it. All those anxieties before the birth were quite unnecessary, although I did find the practical steps I took helped me at the time. **❞**

A lot of fathers are like this one: although anxious about 'feeling right' before the birth, they would probably be amazed if questioned about paternal feelings afterwards. They feel in complete harmony with the situation and never give the matter another thought.

But what about those fathers of young babies who still don't feel that they have been infused with paternal feelings? It's easy for busy and involved fathers to advise not worrying, but not so simple to be feeling rather empty when all around you seem to be deriving great emotional uplift from the arrival of a new baby. Before the birth one can always hope that things will change after the event, but once the child is here then the problem is slightly different.

As suggested earlier, the question for the new father ought to be seen as twofold. First, what are 'paternal feelings'? And second, if I know what they are, can I experience them?

A CHANGE IN STATUS

For many of the fathers questioned, the matter of paternal feelings was closely tied to events after the birth. They felt that their change in status, from having no children to being a father, was what eventually provided them with a range of emotions they were happy to call paternal feelings.

❝ Like many fathers I didn't feel a lot before the birth of our first child. I smiled when other fathers told me how their lives had changed, but I didn't understand what was going to happen at all. But once we had Peter everything seemed different. I compare it with getting promoted at work. At first you are very pleased with life; maybe you've got new colleagues, new responsibilities and a new office. Then you start getting used to the new work and find that a challenge; eventually you take it all in your stride, but feel different inside.

With being a father you find there are lots of new things to get used to, but after a while you come to accept them. But you can never go back to what you were before. You have crossed a threshold. You have responsibilities that won't go away, you are called upon to make important decisions regarding another person, and you always have in the back of your mind the thought that you have to consider somebody else before making major changes to your life. The sum total of this lot, added to all the extra love and joy that there is in your life, somehow adds up to paternal feelings – I think. **❞**

❝ I'd never been passionately in love with my wife – she won't mind me saying that. We knew each other for a long time and just grew together. We are exceptionally happy in life, I should add. Before her I had enjoyed a couple of infatuations with other girls, but nothing too earth-shattering. All in all, therefore, I wasn't really expecting to become terribly over-emotional about the birth of our child. I was, however, hoping to get something special out of it.

As it has turned out, I have a perfect relationship (to my mind) with Theo, but it has come about through getting to know him, not through anything out of the ordinary.

At first I tried to be interested and loving, but frankly found it all a bit of a chore. We soon got to sharing things, however, and as we did so the relationship grew. When he was about two my wife was ill and we spent about three weeks together, with no Mum. There's been no looking back and today, at the age of four, he's my best mate. For me, that's where the paternal feelings come in. It's a relationship built on all the normal rules, getting to like one another, getting to know one another, and doing things together, but of course, there's the extra bit that goes with the fact that I'm his father. That extra bit is where the paternal emotions come into it. **"**

The second father above has formed a very special relationship with his son; at the time of writing, his wife is expecting another baby and both partners have wondered how this is going to affect the paternal feelings that Dad enjoys.

The father below does not have that anxiety – at least, not yet.

" We had been married for ten years before our first child came along. In those years we had seen many of our friends start families and had heard plenty about pregnancies, childbirth, babies and everything else connected with the business. I had always noticed a slight change in the fathers but I could never really define what it was. I always assumed it was the change in responsibility that brought about the change in them.

So when we found out we were having a baby I had this kind of expectation. I was fully prepared to feel different – to feel paternal, or at least to feel like a dad ought. Needless to say nothing much changed for me, and apart from my ever-expanding wife, life went on pretty much as normal. It was only at the birth, and forever thereafter, that the change I had been looking forward to took place. The moment of birth was a much more emotional and exciting moment than I can ever describe. We experienced something more amazing and dramatic than I had ever anticipated. It was if another force was at work, the force of life or God or something. And that has stayed with me ever since – and they are my paternal feelings.

Every time I look at my son I think that my wife and I were

instrumental in putting him on earth, but some greater power played a part too. And for as long as he needs me, I'm charged with the responsibility of protecting him, not for my sake, or even his sake, but because he has been chosen to be born and must be cherished. So my paternal feelings, not simple emotions, are all mixed up with the actual creation of life itself and my responsibility for it. **99**

This father's rather moving definition of what he understands by paternal feelings brings us back to the opening comments. Whatever these feelings are, they're not easy to describe. And if for a time you don't feel right about things, it's probably only a stage of transition. Eventually nearly all fathers find substance in a new relationship with their child. It may come easily before it is born, it may burst on the scene at the same moment as the child or it may grow slowly over the months and years as friendship and affection grow between father and child. Whatever the case, cherish the emotions, and if you wish, call them 'paternal feelings'.

Finally it is worth saying that not all mothers bond with their children from the outset. Some may also experience a sense of something missing and may worry about their ability to be a good mother. This is a factor for fathers to be aware of, especially since, in the eyes of society, a mother with child-relationship difficulties is much less likely to be accepted than a father in the same position. We all expect that mothers will instantly love their children.

WHAT HAPPENS ON THE DAY?

Just as in the movies, the birth of a baby can vary from a mad rush through the dark streets, reaching the hospital with moments to spare, to being a very prolonged affair with much suffering for the mother and pacing about for the father. If, as you read this, you are yet to become a father, then prepare yourself for the unexpected. If you have already experienced a birth then you will have your own personal memory etched into your mind.

As the unpredictability suggests, it's sometimes hard to know when the arrival of a baby is near. There are, of course, some signals but these are not always easy to spot and occasionally they don't give you much warning. However, it can be reassuring to know what's likely to happen, even if in your case your baby doesn't follow the rules.

GETTING STARTED

The mechanisms of childbirth are complex and interesting. It is worthwhile reading about them in some detail. In simple terms you will know when the birth is imminent when your partner starts to experience certain symptoms:

1 A show – this will be a slight loss of blood-stained mucus that has been forming a 'plug' at the cervix.

2 Broken waters – a discharge of fluids coming from ruptured membranes surrounding the baby.

3 Labour pains – occurring because contractions are taking place.

If your partner is a first-time mother then there may be uncertainty about the events. Labour pains will always occur, but the other two parts of the build-up may pass unnoticed or may happen at a later stage. Labour pains may be so mild or unfamiliar that they will be dismissed as indigestion. For some there will be false alarms before labour really begins, while others seem loath to submit to the inevitable and keep convincing themselves that 'this isn't really it'.

The interviews for this book, however, tended to support the popular view that mothers generally know exactly when things are beginning to happen and, despite all the excitement and anticipation, are normally well in tune with their own bodies.

> **❝** I remember at the time we used to describe everything as "our last as just a couple"; we had our last meal out, our last visit to the cinema, our last weekend together. In the event the baby was three weeks late so we ended up with many "lasts". The anticipation did lead to several false alarms, which were probably due to over-excitement and wishful thinking. I did wonder if having the baby was like trying to get yourself off to sleep – the more you tried the harder it became.
> When, at last, labour did really begin Diane looked at me and said: "This is it". I knew from the look on her face that she wasn't joking.
> Having said that, it still took another fourteen hours for the baby to finally arrive. **❞**

The above is typical in many ways. The first baby is more likely to be late, and the labour is frequently longer. Although anything can happen, a typical first labour will be ten to fourteen hours while subsequent children will probably turn up after labours half that length. The 'false alarm' mentioned above is not the same as a 'false labour'. The latter, much more common with second and subsequent children, is a definite burst of contractions. It occurs a week or two before the true labour and is likely to send the parent scurrying off to the hospital.

> **"** We had been given a date by our doctor and a different date by
> the hospital. We knew the doctor well and she kept joking that
> she was right and the hospital was wrong. It became a sort of
> contest to see who would be the closest to the actual day. There
> were several family anniversaries around the time, so uncles and
> cousins were expressing interest too.
>
> All this added to the tension of waiting, and although the baby
> was only two days late it seemed like an eternity. I'm sure some
> people got fed up asking about the arrival because it was "just
> any day now" for about a month. My advice to fathers would be
> to give all their friends and relations a date one week or ten days
> later than the expected one. This will stave off all the questions
> and provide everybody with a nice surprise.
>
> When it did come it was all very straightforward. I remember
> Jilly waking me up at about six in the morning and calmly
> announcing that it would arrive that day. At about two in the
> afternoon she had her first real pains. I came home from work
> and found her experiencing contractions about every twelve
> minutes. We drove off to the hospital, which was only a few
> minutes' drive away, and, presto, had a son about six hours
> later. **"**

The contractions, which may be very painful even at an early stage,
come at regular intervals. You will probably have been given strict
instructions about when to phone your midwife or turn up at the
hospital. The process, for the first-time mother particularly, can be
quite frightening. Most fathers expressed great relief at getting within
reach of medical attention even though, in nearly every case, they
could have stayed at home a few more hours.

Once true labour has started it's not going to stop until the baby is
born. There may be lulls in the contractions, but you're on your way
so it's best to be prepared.

THE MECHANICS OF LABOUR

Labour is divided into three stages.

The *first stage* involves the opening of the cervix to allow the baby's
head to pass through. This stage may take a considerable amount of

time, especially in a first-time mother. The father can be of great assistance during the first stage.

The pain associated with labour begins as the muscles start to contract. Apart from generally offering comfort, the father can help by timing the contractions and informing the medical staff of progress. Additionally he can assist by calmly reminding his partner of the breathing techniques she may have learned, and by helping to reinforce advice given by the medical staff. You may have discussed the 'plan of action' that you and your partner hope to follow during the trying minutes and hours of the first stage of labour. Try to stick to this if possible, but remember that matters tend to get a little impassioned during the labour.

> **❝** I thought it was something of a cliché but I've since realized just how traumatic, for a mother, the labour can be. It was pretty trying for me too. I had never seen my wife in such agony – and I'd never heard her use such words and phrases before, especially not in the company of others! I didn't know what to do to help apart from mildly saying that it would be alright. **❞**

A sense of helplessness was typical amongst fathers. One followed advice recommended in another book.

> **❝** I had read that it was wise to put the contractions in context – in other words, explain their relevance. In practice this entails telling your wife that everything is for a purpose. Every contraction is one gone and one that won't be needed again. The cervix is that little bit wider and the birth is that little bit nearer. Of course it's harder than it sounds, but generally it worked for Pippa and me. She took some grains of comfort from what I was saying, and I felt I was doing something positive. **❞**

For positive action, fathers are recommended to help mothers with their breathing, perhaps assist in the administration of gas-and-air or TENS (see pages 68-70) and make themselves useful about the delivery room. There may well be some quiet moments during the first stage and any activity will help to pass the time and give you and your partner a focus for conversation.

As things hot up during the first stage of labour the pain will intensify and the contractions will become closer together. Some mothers like their partners to aid pain relief by applying pressure to the base of the back (the bones of the sacrum) with their hands. This technique is well known and can give surprisingly good results. It is advisable to read up about this (try *The Expectant Father* by Betty Parsons [Paperfronts]) or attend classes.

In this method the father should press quite hard with the balls of his hands on the sacrum (the mother will know where it feels right) while the woman is either lying on her side or kneeling in front of the man. In the latter case the man and woman will be facing one another in an embrace position.

&& We found it worked very well up to a point, but have to add that the hospital staff were not terribly enthusiastic about it. I felt very good about being involved, but also a bit self-conscious. Jilly had lost all sense of decorum and couldn't have cared less what anybody thought about her screaming at me while I hugged her and forcefully massaged her back. &&

The *second stage* of labour is when the baby is actually pushed through the open cervix to effect the birth. This is clearly the most exciting, and sometimes frightening, period for the woman. All sorts of strange (though natural) things are happening to her body.

As with the first stage you and your partner may have pre-arranged some steps you wish to take. In many cases, however, you will feel a little out of control of events and are left just doing what you can to respond in the best way possible. You will probably be well advised to keep reminding your partner of the breathing requirements and by doing what many fathers suggest – keeping up a running commentary.

&& I had a full view of proceedings and could tell my wife just what was happening. Also, I was in a much better condition than her to hear the advice of the midwife and to try to encourage my wife to follow it. The most exciting moment

during this time was when the top of the baby's head first appeared. I relayed that news to Meg and also described the exciting final seconds as her pushes and screams were translated into the arrival of Junior. I like to think I kept a cool head during the time of the actual birth – but I don't think I did. **99**

The *third stage* is the 'birth' of the afterbirth. Moments after one of the most exhilarating events of her life, your partner will be called upon to undertake just one more bit of work. This is the necessary push to expel the placenta and its membranes. You can be of most value by not forgetting your wife at this moment. Perhaps you can hold the baby to her while the midwife deals with the afterbirth, or perhaps you can comfort her while baby is being cleaned up and she is thinking ahead to her well-earned rest.

The first stage of labour will be the longest and hardest, but you must not underestimate the problems of the second and third stages. You should always listen to the midwife about when to push and when to hold on, reinforcing this piece of information to your wife. And most of all you must try to do the impossible, namely understand exactly what your partner is going through. There is no room for selfishness on the part of the father in the delivery room.

A last comment on the business of labour can be left to one of the fathers. His approach can counterbalance some of the more austere-sounding pieces of advice given above.

66 It was only a day or two before the birth, burdened down as we were with every kind of advice that you could wish to receive, when Pam pointed out that it could all be rather enjoyable. Hearing about pain relief, labour, stitches and so on had led us to believe that it was going to be rather gruelling. The only positive words used were "joy" and "unity" – it all sounded rather like going to church.

So Pam and I decided to try to enjoy it. And to a certain extent we succeeded. We were able to keep joking up to the last and shared the magical moments with a light heart, not a totally serious one. I think we were lucky to feel the way we did; just being positive helped us no end. **99**

PREPARATIONS FOR THE DAY

Perhaps the most important thing is to have some knowledge of what to expect. There are many myths about childbirth and knowing the facts can be a comfort to you and your partner. Once you know what's likely to happen you can plan accordingly and be left free to enjoy the excitement rather than be worried by it. An apparently calm partner, even if you're terrified inside, can be very reassuring for the woman.

66 Our main problem was my work. I used to travel quite long distances on an almost daily basis and so didn't know where I would be on the day. Because so many friends had produced babies either weeks early or weeks late it didn't seem possible to pick just one week off for holiday and hope that that would be the week. Anyway, I was saving some holiday for when we were first home with the baby.

I wanted to be there but had no idea whether it would be possible or not. For about ten days I was constantly phoning home to ask if there was any news. My customers got quite used to me asking to use their phones, and this taught me one lesson – people love a birth. When I explained that my wife was due any minute and could I call home, the response was always so positive. Some customers whom I visited on only a six-monthly basis still remembered and asked about the child on my next visit. I always tell my colleagues, half in jest and half truthfully, that being an "expectant" dad was the best selling tool I ever had.

In the event the baby turned up on a Sunday, so I didn't have an exciting story to tell of dashing back from Rotherham to get there just in time. **99**

Of course, planning to get father to the birth is not as important as preparing the way for mother. But assuming that all eventualities are covered for her – if the car breaks down, if you don't own a telephone, if the hospital is sixty miles away – then it is certainly worth making a few contingency plans.

As the father above suggested, you will enjoy a temporarily elevated status as an 'expectant' dad, particularly if it's your first child.

You might as well enjoy the situation. A member of the armed forces who was interviewed recounted that he was away on a particularly important course when his first child was due. His knowledge of army life suggested that it was not even worth requesting leave, but the prospect of a new arrival in the world softened the necessary hearts. He was out on an assault course when he was suddenly ordered home to attend to his wife – and to be quick about it!

If you want to be present at the birth, and more about that in a later section, then do make a few plans to make sure you will be able to do so. Although it's true that most children are born at night, it could be your luck to be stranded miles from home on a weekday morning when your first child arrives.

TAKE CARE

Having prepared for what might happen, and having taught yourself about the likely signs, there is little else to say except to sound a warning note. It is a fact that childbirth is a major upheaval to the woman's body. Complications can occur with the birth. You may not want to appear to be a hypochondriac, but if in doubt, phone the hospital or the midwife (whichever you have previously arranged).

You may be surprised at just how much importance the medical profession places on achieving happy and successful births. They will take every precaution to ensure that the baby and mother are safe and well, and so every call and enquiry you make will be treated with the utmost seriousness, especially if you are first-time parents. Never be afraid to call to express any anxieties or problems you may be experiencing. In the vast majority of cases the birth of a child goes smoothly and well, but don't take any chances. It's not worth the risk.

COULD WE COPE WITH A MISCARRIAGE?

YOU'RE NOT ALONE

Miscarriages are very common. This information will not lessen the sense of loss, but it may have one very positive benefit.

" We were very shocked by the miscarriage, because everything had been going so well. I can't think what was the worst part of it, but it may have just been the fact that we badly wanted a child.

We had told everybody about the pregnancy and so had to tell everybody about the loss of the child. There seemed no other way of doing it but simply to come out with the news when anyone asked us, as they did all the time, about the baby. It was then that we discovered that so many other people had first- or second-hand experience of miscarriage. We had never known that many of our close friends, and even one relation, had either lost babies in this way or at least had close knowledge of others who had. It turned out to be a great comfort, particularly for my wife. She, understandably, was very upset and found it helpful to talk to other women who had been through the same trauma. **"**

This father-to-be was surprised by the news that so many of his friends had close knowledge of miscarriages. The reason for his surprise is that, when you happily announce your pregnancy, the last thing people are going to say is: 'Great news, we once had a miscarriage.' So it becomes something of a secret, revealed only when people need the information. Perhaps the lesson to be learned is to talk about your unfortunate experience; you may find comfort and understanding from unexpected quarters. It is thought that as many as one in five pregnancies ends in some kind of miscarriage, so there is a good chance that somebody close to you will know just what you are suffering.

That a couple can take some kind of comfort from sharing their sad news suggests that talking is good therapy. Talking within the relationship is very important, too. For obvious biological reasons the woman feels the loss much more keenly than the man. That is when she will need to feel that she has somebody on whom she can rely totally. This father-to-be was very honest and open about what happened in his life.

> Pauline had the miscarriage when I was at work. Nobody called me; I just came home to find my sister-in-law with my wife. They told me what had happened and my sister-in-law left us to be together. I didn't know how to handle the situation. I had not really taken much part in the pregnancy so far and I don't think the sense of loss, for me, was very great. I had read that miscarriages are common and that they rarely have any effect on the woman's ability to bear children later.
>
> Pauline and I chatted and I made her a cup of tea. I suggested she went back to bed, and we discussed when the doctor was next going to see her. It all seemed so matter-of-fact, like having a sprained ankle or something. The impact was minimal on me, so much so in fact that I went out later that evening, went back to work the next day and carried on as if nothing much had happened.
>
> A few weeks later I came home to find Pauline's sister round again. Pauline had completely cracked up; she had been crying all day. There was nothing I could do. She wouldn't talk to me at all and eventually it was decided that she should go to stay with her sister for a short while. These few days gave me time to think about my attitude.

When Pauline came back I tried to do all the talking and comforting that I should have done some weeks before. It was too late. I have to say that things have not been the same since, even though she's now pregnant. She keeps asking if I really want this baby. In the circumstances this is a fair question. I'm sure that matters will improve after the birth when we will have a baby to take our minds off the past. If my experience is anything to go by, the father must not underestimate the immense emotional strain, for a woman, of a miscarriage. **"**

The sense of loss for the woman may be greater than that caused simply by the physical act of miscarriage. The later the miscarriage occurs then the greater the likelihood of her having become used to being the centre of attention. Medical staff, family and friends are all taking a keen interest in her health and her progress, and all are looking forward to a magical date some five, six or seven months ahead. The loss of the baby means that suddenly that is all gone. Some people may find it hard to talk to her for a while after the miscarriage and may keep their distance, ironically at a time when she may need their attention most. It all adds up to an extremely wretched time for a woman, a time when she most needs the support of her partner.

At the same time as the father-to-be is providing the support his partner obviously needs, he will also be coping with his own emotions. Talking with other men with similar experiences can be a great help. Men are often accused of failing to show their emotions, especially to other men. Whether generally true or not, the experience of the men interviewed at a time of miscarriage certainly did not bear this out. They were happy to talk and to share.

Providing even the simplest care has been taken over the care of the pregnant woman, there should be absolutely no sense of guilt attached to a miscarriage. That your partner was still working or that you had said you weren't looking forward to changing all those nappies will not have caused a miscarriage. The important thing is to get over the event as quickly as possible.

WHAT NEXT?

It is essential, of course, that your partner sees her doctor at the time of a miscarriage. It is a good idea for the couple to attend a later appointment too, when the doctor can tell you in specific terms how you stand with regard to trying for another baby – should that be your decision. The doctor will probably not discuss the cause of the miscarriage. The reason for this is that there may not be any discernible reason why the baby was 'naturally aborted', and even if there were, it might be of no relevance to the future. There are numerous possible causes for a miscarriage, ranging from illness in the mother to abnormalities in the foetus possibly caused by the father being elderly. There are very few general rules, however, that can be applied to this particular area because research into the problem has proved inconclusive. Your doctor may recommend for your partner a D & C (dilation and curettage) which is one of the commonest gynaecological operations performed. The reason for this course of action is that fragments of the placenta and foetus may still be in the womb; the D & C will clear them out. This operation is normally carried out under general anaesthetic and will leave your partner in need of a short period of convalescence.

For couples who have experienced a miscarriage there is sometimes an understandable need to look for a cause.

CC We wanted a child and so began trying again just a few months after the first miscarriage. The doctor saw no reason why we should not be completely successful. She said that the fact that we had conceived once showed that we had no problems in that area and so should have no trouble next time.

Maura actually fell pregnant very quickly, but it was not like the first time. This time we were so careful with everything. Maura gave up work immediately and used to spend a good part of every day resting. We watched her diet, banned everyone from smoking in the house and cut down drastically on all our social engagements. The worst aspect was that we racked our brains to try to come up with a reason for the first miscarriage. We relived the actual day so many times to see if there was something that had triggered off the loss of the baby. I don't think that either of us felt guilty about the first miscarriage, but we would have done if we had missed something that had contributed to it.

Funnily enough, I think we knew all along that there was no fault on our part, but it became something of an obsession. Maura gave up eating certain foods and stopped driving because she wondered if the seats in the car caused her to sit incorrectly.

We never did find any cause for the first miscarriage and were successful with our second pregnancy. My only thoughts now are just how dreadful it would have been, after all the effort we put in, had we lost the second baby too. **"**

Looking for causes that don't exist can cause extra anxiety and put unnecessary pressure on the woman carrying a child for the second time. For the father-to-be the only advice must be to try to allay any fears that your partner has. Unless somebody has been grossly neglectful or totally reckless, there should be no guilt attached to a miscarriage. There will be enough unhappiness without adding to it with other negative emotions.

Fortunately, many parents-to-be cope with the loss by a rationalization of events. Those with religious convictions frequently find some meaning in the miscarriage, while others believe that the body has aborted the foetus for good reasons, such as a potential problem later for either the mother or the child. One has to cope, and there must be validity in any method that encourages the process. An excellent guide to the subject, and one that is sympathetic to the sense of loss experienced by the father as well as the mother, is *Miscarriage* by Oakley, McPherson and Roberts (Fontana Paperbacks).

Finally, it is worth saying at this point that some pregnancies end with a medical abortion, some with a stillbirth and some in a successful delivery but with the child dying hours or days afterwards. In such situations talking and grieving do, eventually, help. It is to be hoped that anyone unfortunate enough to suffer such a dreadful experience can find someone or something that will give them the strength to recover.

THE LANGUAGE OF PREGNANCY AND CHILDBIRTH

Some 'expectant' fathers complained of feeling left out of discussions about pregnancy and childbirth. Their partners, particularly when in discussion with other women, would be fluent in a completely new language – one that was unknown to the fathers. This situation is hardly surprising when you remember that most of the education is aimed at women. And if you have decided not to attend classes, and you don't fancy wading through a large medical tome, you are likely to remain largely unfamiliar with this new range of terms.

This short glossary contains those that seem to occur most commonly. The explanations should be enough to help you understand them and their usage. More extensive explanations can be found, of course, in some of the large medically based books dealing with pregnancy and childbirth.

AFTERBIRTH is the placenta and the membranes which are delivered after the baby.

AMNIOCENTESIS is the test of the amniotic fluid which can be taken normally between the fourteenth and the sixteenth week of pregnancy. It detects abnormalities of the foetal central nervous system (such as spina bifida) and some form of mental handicap (such as Down's syndrome). In some areas it is offered routinely to all pregnant women over thirty-five years old, but as there is a 0.5–1% risk of miscarriage as a result of the test, women are asked to agree beforehand to a termination of the pregnancy should any abnormalities be found. The procedure is uncomfortable: a fine hollow tube is inserted through the woman's abdominal wall below the umbilicus into the uterus – ultrasound scanning helps to position it away from the foetus. The fluid is then sucked up through the needle for testing. The baby's sex can also be determined with this test.

AMNIOTIC FLUID surrounds the foetus within the membranes. It is composed of approximately 98.8% water and 1.2% solid matter, and the amount of it varies during pregnancy, peaking at about 500–1500ml at 35 weeks. The foetus both absorbs and excretes the fluid.

ANAEMIA, a reduced concentration of red cells in the blood, is a fairly common complaint during pregnancy because of the increased demands on the woman's body. Usually it is simply a matter of iron and folic acid deficiency, which can be put right by tablets (these unfortunately can contribute to constipation).

ANAESTHESIA is defined as 'reversible depression of the senses', in which state the woman should be incapable of feeling pain. It does not necessarily mean total unconsciousness; this happens only under a general anaesthetic. If this is needed during labour, the father is likely to be excluded from the delivery.

AN ANALGESIC is a drug, such as morphine and pethidine, which can relieve pain without producing unconsciousness (see page 69).

APGAR SCORES reflect the condition of the newborn infant in the first minutes of life. They are a numerical assessment of the baby's heartbeat, colour, breathing, muscle tone and his/her response to having the foot flicked. In some places, Apgar scores are supplemented by temperature readings.

BIRTHMARKS sometimes cause concern; they are usually small pinkish areas on the nape of the neck or the eyelids and almost always disappear within a few weeks. Strawberry marks grow after delivery and usually go by the sixth birthday; moles are left alone for later treatment if necessary. Port wine stain, a major purple discoloration, will also be treated later.

BRAXTON-HICKS CONTRACTIONS are painless (generally) contractions of the uterus which occur from about the 20th week of pregnancy onwards. Towards the end of the pregnancy they can be felt quite strongly and may be mistaken for the real thing – hence the expression 'false labour'.

BREATHING isn't a simple matter, especially during labour. This is the reason why breathing techniques may form a significant part of any lessons you may attend.

BREECH DELIVERY happens when the baby arrives bottom first or feet first instead of head first. A breech presentation (position) often means a long labour and because of this, and possible problems with the cord, some breech babies are delivered by Caesarean section.

CAESAREAN SECTION offers an alternative for those mothers and babies for whom the orthodox route poses too many problems. A Caesarean section is much better for both of them than a very difficult vaginal delivery. The incision is below the bikini line; the uterus is opened and the waters are sucked out (a disconcerting noise); then the baby is delivered and the cord cut. The afterbirth is removed, and everything else is packed back into place and the wound is closed. Most hospitals encourage women to have epidural or spinal block anaesthesia and allow partners to be present – do be there if you can. Fathers attending Caesarean births found it was not too nasty if they sat at the head end and concentrated on their partner! Extra rest is recommended for women who have a Caesarean section.

THE CERVIX is sometimes called 'the neck of the womb'. It is the lowest third of the uterus and separates the business end of the uterus from the vagina. During labour it opens (dilates) to 10cm to allow the baby through the birth canal.

COLOSTRUM is the earliest milk from the mother. It contains extra goodness for the newborn infant, especially as it gives some immunity to disease, and is higher in protein than normal maternal milk.

THE CONFINEMENT is the having-the-baby time.

CONTRACTIONS used to be called 'labour pains'. The uterus changes from being a protective environment for the developing foetus into a gigantic muscle which tightens, or contracts, to open and draw up the cervix. This forms the birth canal.

THE CROWNING is the arrival of the baby's head, seen emerging from the vagina.

DILATION or DILATING is the process of opening of the cervix to form part of the birth canal.

EPIDURAL ANAESTHESIA is a method of pain relief which enables the woman to remain fully conscious but unaware of sensation below the position of the needle (see page 70).

AN EPISIOTOMY is the surgical cutting of the perineum to allow the baby's head easier passage and to prevent tearing, which would be harder to repair.

FALSE LABOUR is when Braxton-Hicks contractions are mistaken for the onset of real labour. A woman who makes this error will probably be very disappointed and rather ashamed (quite unnecessarily so), so do be sympathetic. Maternity units are used to dummy runs, so it is not a problem to anyone!

FOETAL DISTRESS in labour means that the baby is experiencing some physical difficulty and the medical staff will consider what should be done to improve matters. It is usually detected by a foetal monitor, by the midwife listening to the foetal heart, or by meconium in the waters.

FOETAL MONITORS may be used throughout the labour. Both foetal breathing and foetal heartbeat can be monitored through a transducer strapped to the mother's abdomen.

THE FOETUS is the unborn baby, from the second month of pregnancy to delivery.

THE FONTANELLES are the gappy, spongy bits of the baby's skull. The head is designed to alter shape during its journey through the mother's pelvis, and the fontanelles are soft to allow this to happen. The skull hardens up in about eighteen months.

FORCEPS DELIVERY happens when the baby can't manage to emerge unaided. There are various types of forceps, for use in different situations. The woman is put into the lithotomy position and the forceps – sometimes described as 'giant sugar tongs' – are slid into position around the baby's head. The baby is then assisted out, ideally combined with the mother's own expulsive efforts.

GAS-AND-AIR or INHALATION ANALGESIA is a self-administered method of pain relief (see page 69).

GUTHRIE TEST is performed on the six-day-old infant. The heel is scratched and blood is dripped on to circles on a card; this enables the diagnosis of phenylketonuria, which leads to severe mental retardation, to be made.

GYNAECOLOGISTS are doctors specializing in disorders of women's reproductive organs. They may take a hand in the pregnancy if specific problems are affecting the woman.

'HEAD ENGAGED' is the expression used to describe the baby's head settling down into the pelvic brim ready for the start of labour. It is noticed particularly in the first-time mother.

'HIGH-TECH' DELIVERY implies that technology has taken over – as far away as you can get from natural childbirth.

HYPERTENSION is high blood pressure which, if untreated, may lead in extreme cases to pre-eclampsia; rest is recommended, salt is restricted and weight gain is very carefully checked.

HYPERVENTILATION is excessive fast shallow breathing which prevents carbon dioxide from being expelled from the lungs, thus depriving the foetus of oxygen. So don't let your partner get too carried away.

HYPNOSIS can work as a method of pain relief for properly prepared women. Preparation needs to start fairly early in pregnancy; some GPs actively encourage this.

INDUCED LABOUR usually happens only when the anticipated date of arrival is well past or when there are problems with continued pregnancy. Sometimes it is sufficient for the waters to be broken; otherwise a drip of artificial hormone, which stimulates the hormones into action, is inserted into the woman's arm, or a hormone pessary is put in the vagina.

LABOUR is the process by which the baby is born. There are three stages of labour:

   i   the contractions, by which the cervix dilates and is drawn up to form part of the birth canal;
   ii the expulsive effort to deliver the baby;
   iii the delivery of the placenta and membranes.

Some authorities give a fourth stage, for the hour following the delivery of the placenta, when there is the greatest risk of post-partum haemorrhage (excessive bleeding).

LANUGO is fine hair which covers the foetal body by the twenty-eighth week of pregnancy. It has usually disappeared by the thirty-eighth week, but may sometimes be seen on newborn babies, especially across the shoulders.

LIGHTENING is when the uterus actually drops down a bit into the pelvis, and the foetus sinks into the uterus – the head may engage ready for labour to start. The woman can breathe more comfortably, and if she has suffered from indigestion, that should get better – but she will probably need to visit the loo even more frequently.

LITHOTOMY POSITION is necessary for a forceps delivery, with the mother's feet raised in stirrups while she lies supine on the delivery bed.

LOCHIA is the discharge of blood and debris from the uterus following the delivery of the baby. It continues for several weeks.

MECONIUM is the first sticky greenish bowel movements of the newborn. It can last for several days. If it appears in the waters during labour it may be a sign of foetal distress.

MEMBRANES are the bag holding the waters round the baby. Usually, in labour they're referred to as in 'rupturing the membranes' or 'breaking the waters'.

THE MIDWIFE will manage most of the labour and may be male.

MONITORS may be used during labour. One of these is used to indicate the build-up of the contractions; others reflect the condition of the foetus.

THE NCT (NATIONAL CHILDBIRTH TRUST) is an organization dedicated to 'education for parenthood'. It tends to emphasize natural childbirth and breast-feeding, and does much valuable work through both ante-natal classes and post-natal support groups.

NATURAL CHILDBIRTH is the term publicized by Grantly Dick-Read, who believed that childbirth could, and should, be free of pain and fear; as early as the 1920s he established classes for women and their partners to prepare them for childbirth.

AN OBSTETRICIAN is a doctor who specializes in caring for pregnant women and their babies. Your partner will see him at regular intervals during the ante-natal stage and he may be present for the actual birth of your baby.

OEDEMA is swelling; often the ankles swell during pregnancy (about 40% of pregnant women suffer this during the last twelve weeks). Sometimes the swelling spreads up the legs, or affects the hands. It may indicate high blood pressure or pre-eclampsia, so should be reported to the midwife.

A PAEDIATRICIAN is a doctor who specializes in treatment of childhood diseases. Paediatricians normally work in hospitals and one will probably check on your baby soon after its birth. This check will be immediate if there were any complications with the birth.

PERINEUM is the muscular area separating the vagina from the anus. It is subject to a lot of stress during the delivery of the baby and if it seems unlikely to 'give' enough, an episiotomy may be performed.

PHOTOTHERAPY is a means of helping a jaundiced baby.

THE PLACENTA is an organ that grows to the size of a dinner plate. It is embedded into the inner surface of the uterus, usually somewhere in the upper half. The surface of the placenta not attached to the uterus is covered with membranes which line the rest of the uterus and form the bag containing the foetus. The foetus is in the amniotic fluid, connected to the placenta (and thence to the mother) through the umbilical cord. The placenta thus links the foetus and mother and filters the nourishment the foetus receives, though most drugs, including antibiotics, nicotine and alcohol, can 'cross the placenta' and affect the baby.

PLACENTA PRAEVIA is the condition where the placenta, instead of being attached to the upper part of the uterus, comes to lie partially or completely over the cervix. In severe cases a Caesarean section then becomes necessary because of the bleeding that would otherwise result if the cervix dilated.

POSTERIOR POSITION of the baby is when the foetus has its backbone curled up against the mother's backbone, instead of its backbone curled up against the outside of the tummy. This indicates that a long labour is likely. Sometimes the foetus shifts itself around during labour; it may be moved by the medical staff; or it may just be awkward. It can lead to difficulty in delivery as the baby's head is not in the best position to push through.

POST-NATAL DEPRESSION is a clinical condition which seems to be hormonal in origin. Most women get weepy five or six days after delivery but this is not defined as post-natal depression, which is much more serious. If you're in doubt, get professional help – doctors, midwives and health visitors are aware of the problem, so use them. The depression is discussed in the next section of the book.

PRE-ECLAMPSIA, PRE-ECLAMPSIA TOXAEMIA or PET occurs in 5–10% of all pregnancies. The blood pressure rises, fluid is retained and eventually protein will be detected in the urine. This threatens the well-being of the foetus, as well as the mother, so any indications that it could be on the cards are dealt with immediately.

THE PUERPERIUM is the period, some six weeks, following the birth of the baby.

'SCABU' is the SPECIAL CARE BABY UNIT which is available at the larger regional hospitals. The staff are specially trained to care for sick or premature babies and their parents. Babies in need of highly specialized care will be referred there.

SEDATIVE drugs relieve anxiety and encourage calmness and drowsiness. Like all drugs, sedatives can 'cross the placenta' and affect the baby.

THE SHOW is one of the indications that labour is starting; it is the appearance of some blood and the mucus plug which has sealed the cervix, protecting the uterus from possible infection through the vagina during pregnancy.

SPINAL-BLOCK ANAESTHESIA involves local anaesthetic being inserted into a different part of the spinal column from an epidural. It cannot be topped up, unlike an epidural, and it is also not always fully effective.

STRETCH MARKS are silvery marks on the skin, which occur as the abdomen expands. There are various preparations on the market which are supposed to prevent them, but these are usually not effective.

TENS is the abbreviated form of TRANS-ELECTRONIC NERVE STIMULATION – a form of self-administered pain relief (see page 70).

A TRANQUILLIZER relieves anxiety and generally acts as a sedative, though it may not cause drowsiness.

ULTRASOUND or ULTRASONIC SCAN is usually administered from about the twelfth week of pregnancy as an aid to the accurate dating of the pregnancy and as a check on the health of the foetus. The abdomen is smeared with a jelly-like substance and the probe is rubbed over it, bombarding the sides with ultrasonic energy. This bounces back off the foetus and its image is projected on to the screen, though it needs a trained observer to know what's what. It is very helpful if the bladder is full before an ultrasound, but this is the only discomfort experienced by the woman – though there is some concern that the technique may possibly distress the foetus.

ULTRASONIC FOETAL PULSE DETECTORS use the same basic technique as ultrasound but are wired up to produce the sound of the foetal heartbeat.

THE UMBILICAL CORD is the lifeline which connects the foetus to the mother. It is still working throughout labour and delivery. Once the baby has arrived, the cord is cut and its stub is clipped or tied on the baby's tummy. Eventually this rather unsightly bit drops off – and there's a belly button.

UTERUS is another word for the womb. It has a dual role, as an organ which shelters the placenta – and the foetus – and as a muscle which expels the foetus and the placenta at the appropriate time.

THE VENTOUSE or VACUUM EXTRACTOR provides an alternative to forceps delivery, with a suction cup fitted to the baby's head while still in the birth canal. The vacuum-cleaner principle then applies.

VERNIX is the sticky substance covering the baby. It has been likened in texture to cream cheese and has been protecting the foetus from its watery environment in the past few months. It soon comes off.

THE WATERS are the amniotic fluid in which the foetus has developed.

2

THE EARLY WEEKS AND MONTHS

DIFFERENT – BUT HOW DIFFERENT?

One of the few aspects of fatherhood that is held to be universally true – perhaps the only point on which everyone will agree – is that your life will never be the same again. If you are an expectant father you will doubtless have been on the receiving end of pitying glances from a tired-looking father who tells you just this with a voice full of dread. Don't worry about him; he was the same about marriage when talking to engaged friends, and will be the same again if you tell him you've bought a second-hand car. Don't, however, assume that his message is not accurate. Life after children *is* very different. The question is, just how different?

There are of course the obvious things, such as having more people in the home than before and your partner no longer being pregnant. But there are also large areas of your life that will alter slightly but significantly, changes that will take place that you probably could not have anticipated, and differences in attitudes and emotions that will surprise you. Some of these are looked at in some detail later in this section of the book, but below are some of the more general points that fathers found different about their new lives. Reading what they have to say may help you to understand those pitying glances a little better.

A LIFE RESCHEDULED

❝ The baby soon established its own timetable of events. It slept at certain hours, wanted feeding at certain times and was available for cooing and cuddles on a strict two-hours-per-day rota. To be honest, Harry didn't have it all his own way. The new scheme of things was something of a compromise between Harry and us. We always tried to have him in bed by seven at night, even if this meant that he cried himself to sleep. In return, we would happily get up at six in the morning to give him a change and early feed.

There were numerous other changes because of the baby. For example, we would often eat lunch together because I could come home from work. We would have this at about midday since Harry was asleep then; had we waited an hour we would have been trying to eat our lunch while feeding and changing him at the same time. **"**

Other fathers had many similar examples. Visits to the shops, to other people's homes or just round the corner were planned not to affect the baby's sleep. Car trips, on which babies frequently fall asleep, were assiduously avoided near bedtime in case this would result in a wakeful night. Bedtimes were another aspect of life that often changed – early nights to compensate for lost sleep, or early mornings to feed the baby were very common. And so on. The degree to which you allow the baby's timetable to affect your own is a matter of choice, but most fathers found that a few rescheduled meals and a few delayed journeys were a small price to pay for a baby with a good routine.

Of course, young babies do sleep a lot, both during the day and, hopefully, during the night. In your rescheduled life these moments when baby is asleep will be treasured and utilized to the full. They may not, however, be quite what you expected.

" Some strange things just went completely by the board. I used to read a daily newspaper, every day, from cover to cover. Since Carly was born I normally end up crawling into bed at about eleven at night with an unopened daily paper. My wife, Jessie, and I used to spend some time every day sitting round the kitchen table talking about things over a cup of coffee. That time seems to have disappeared too. Whenever Carly is asleep there seem to be too many things to do to

allow us to sit down and read or chat. And as for sleeping in **"**
at the weekend . . ..

As suggested by the last father, the little luxuries are often the
things that go. There is simply less time in the day to fit in all
that you used to do. Fathers cut down on nights out, weekend
sporting events, hobbies in the home and several other previously
enjoyed activities.

Everything that has been said so far sounds like hard work,
and that's just what it is. Most fathers of young children found
that they were more tired as a result of the new arrival. Much of
this was put down to sleepless nights, but others complained of
the pressure to help out when they wanted to be resting. If you
have been away from home working all week you may fondly
hope for some relaxation when you get home. If your partner has
been looking after your child all this time she may look forward
to your homecoming to give her a break. Nothing more need be
said about this potentially difficult situation.

The father-to-be may perhaps be excused for thinking that too
much is being made of all these trifles. Organizing three people
cannot, surely, be much more work that organizing two.

" We were both determined to work hard at bringing up our
children in the best possible way, but we didn't want them
to dominate our lives. We had too many friends who
seemed to be totally consumed by their children to want to
fall into that trap. One solution, we thought, was to try to
get the children to fit in with our lives as much as possible.
When our first child came along I tried to practise what we
had preached. Whenever I went out, to go to the shops,
work in the garden or just to visit a friend, I would suggest
taking Annabel. It soon became a big drag for me and my
wife. To take a baby out in a car takes about twenty
minutes' preparation, getting her changed, dressed in warm
clothes and sat in her baby seat. An extra bottle, nappy and
clothes for emergencies were also needed – and I had to try
to get her back in time for her next sleep. I once spent half
an hour getting her all ready to spend about ten minutes in
the garden. It's a big chore. **"**

This business of preparation can quickly affect the concept of 'just popping out'. Trips need to be planned in advance or made by only one partner. Your social life can also take a hammering, although most fathers went to elaborate steps to protect this part of their lives. More about this later.

To go on about the extra effort and pressure can present an unrealistically gloomy picture. Your domestic arrangements may mean you do little of the work connected with the baby and you may, therefore, find your life largely unaffected. Alternatively, you may thrive on the extra work, finding that it fills a void in your life. But however events turn out, you will probably find that your relationship with your partner is affected by the birth of your baby. Before looking at the positive gains the birth can bring, this section covers some of the negative points raised.

PRESSURE ON THE RELATIONSHIP

❝ We never argued so much as when Jesse was young. It was entirely predictable, I suppose. Neither of us wanted to admit it but we both found it hard to give up our personal time to change nappies and nurse a crying baby. Jesse was not the easiest of children anyway, having quite a bit of sickness.

The only saving grace was that we didn't turn our anger against the baby, although from time to time I got pretty close to it. Looking back now, the rows all followed an entirely predictable format and may even have been useful in helping us let off steam. **❞**

With many tense situations it's possible to deal with the problem that is causing the friction. With a baby, that can be very difficult. The infant, with its demands and whims, cannot easily be ignored. Many fathers said that the weeks and months after the birth of their first child were both the best and the worst they could remember. The best, because of the thrill of having a new family member; the worst because of the fraught relationship with their wife or partner. The good news was that, almost without exception, matters improved as the baby grew older – although not necessarily *because* the baby grew older.

Family arguments, of course, are not simple matters. There's normally more at stake than just the outcome of the verbal battle. But it might help to remember that the reasons for arguing about who made baby's milk too hot, or who woke baby up by banging the door shut, are not part of the regular power struggle that exists. There's extra pressure on the two parents: both may be tired, short of sleep or money, and both may be silently regretting a missed trip to the cinema or night out with friends.

The father may be in a better position to make the first moves to reconciliation and a happier way forward. He has neither experienced the physical upheaval, with attendant hormonal changes, that has affected the mother, nor is he likely to be so tied to the baby, perhaps getting away from the home on a daily basis.

> **❝** The only time I've ever seen Melanie really cry was about two months after Jamie's birth. We had been arguing on a daily basis and it was getting us both down. It was only when we spoke about things that I think I realized that she felt differently from me. I had previously assumed that we shared the same feelings of frustration and entrapment but, after talking to her, I realized that she felt a growing sense of claustrophobia. She was desperate to leave the house, the baby and me behind. So this was arranged, and it made the world of difference.
>
> She had been driven to a frank admission of her unhappiness by feeling so low. I was sorry that things had had to get so bad before they could get better – but relieved that things were said. **❞**

Some other fathers recognized similar situations in their homes and wished too that they could have suggested some pressure-relieving excursion for the mother before matters got too bad. Some thought that a trip away from the baby for both partners might be a good idea. Some mothers may need persuading that they should not feel guilty about wanting to be away from their young child, while others may genuinely not feel they need a break. It is to be hoped that you will know your own partner well enough to help her make her decision at a time when emotions may be running high and physical reserves are running low.

CROSSING THE THRESHOLD

So far, the picture of your changing life may be rather gloomy. Before we move on to the good news, of which there is plenty, there are a few observations from fathers about their altering lifestyle that can best be described as 'neutral'.

> **"** We felt we were "crossing over" when we had children. Although we had been married for several years before Zak came along, it was his birth that marked the real change in our lives. Apart from going out a lot less, which was an immediate change, we found the range of our friends changing. We spent more time with couples with kids than previously and saw a lot less of some of our single friends. **"**

It's easy to think that you will not be in the same position, and that you will not let the birth of your child affect your life that much. Often, however, it's not your attitude that is the crucial factor. You may find that you feel much more comfortable sharing times with people who understand your need to jump up from a meal to comfort your baby, or who will put up with a crying child because they know that you can't spend all day cuddling and feeding him. In practical terms, too, it's much easier to visit a home that is already geared up to children. Naturally, the degree of change is still largely under your control, but when single friends suddenly want to pop out for a quick drink or watch that late-night movie, you may feel a little left out.

Some fathers felt that changing friends was only a small part of a bigger change that was taking place. And whereas changing friends may affect both partners equally, this broader change seemed to affect fathers more than their partners.

> **❝** It was at the first family gathering after Fran's birth that I realized the importance of a new generation starting. I had always been at the bottom end of the family scale with my grandparents at the top and my parents in the middle. First my grandparents died (one lived to see Fran), and then Fran was born. I had been moved up to take a position in the middle of the family.
>
> At the same time as this I was making a will reflecting the new arrival, and was being looked on more and more as the one in the family who would take decisions for my mother and father in their old age. **❞**

Again we see the sense of 'crossing over' some sort of threshold. Naturally this may not occur overnight, but will probably be a gradual process. Family occasions will be interesting moments at which to mark the passing of time and the subtle alteration in your status.

Not every father will belong to a wider family as described above, but the change will probably be noticeable within the small family unit created by the new arrival. A new sense of responsibility, to your partner and child, may help bring about the transformation although, interestingly, few fathers mentioned feeling any burden of responsibility. The need to nurture and assist, in whatever way, the progress of one's child seemed to be such an obvious responsibility – one that had normally been accepted well before its birth – that it remained unstated as an important change in the father's life.

THE GOOD NEWS

Much of this section, and indeed much of the book, deals with the difficult bits about being a first-time father. The reason for this is that the author and those fathers interviewed hope to help new fathers over these difficulties so that they can enjoy a happy and satisfying period of parenthood. Much, indeed most, of being a father is not difficult. It's fun and it's fulfilling. Apart from the fact that the book would be three times as long if it dealt with all the positive aspects, it's also much better to experience these good things than to read about them. Just to balance this chapter, however, it's worth recording some of the positive points that fathers mentioned, particularly those that came unexpectedly.

66 We laughed so much more. I can remember as a child, and even into my early twenties, I would sometimes laugh quite uncontrollably. I seemed to lose that knack as I got older . . . but it all came back when Russell was born. The silliest things, and he did the silliest things, would crease us up. **99**

66 I learned patience. Before Chris was born I had a very short fuse and could never do things quickly enough. With Chris there were certain things that just had to take time. In adults I couldn't understand why people were sometimes so slow or dithery, but Chris taught me helplessness and I learned the lesson. People have actually commented on my improved nature! I must have been horribly intolerant before. **99**

66 I've gained two extra hours per day in that I now get up every morning at six o'clock. Had I been asked to do this of my own free will I would have complained and said I needed my eight hours per night. Because of the baby I'm up with the lark and haven't felt so fit and well in years. **99**

66 I now watch films at three in the morning that I would have missed otherwise! **99**

Serious or not, the good parts about your changed lifestyle will far outweigh the problems. And should you need reminding, this father tells us about the major gain that sometimes gets overlooked.

66 What I got was a friend – someone who needs and trusts me, someone I can go to football matches with, someone who smiles when I tickle him and cries if I go out in the car without him, a pal who rushes into my room every morning and pulls my glasses off my nose when I'm trying to read a paper. I got someone so dear to me that I cry tears of joy when I look at him asleep in his cot at night. I got a son. **"**

WHAT ABOUT THE FIRST FEW DAYS?

The first few days after the birth of your child are very special for you, your partner and, of course for your son or daughter. They can, however, also be days fraught with tension and problems. This is very unfortunate, but perhaps not unexpected in a situation where too many people are often trying to do too many things.

HOSPITAL VISITING

Assuming that you are not having your child at home, then the first days will be spent visiting your new family.

❝ During the day I was at work and so Jenny's friends would go in and see her and the baby. Many of them worked at the hospital anyway so Jenny felt quite at home. In the evening I would be there from the moment the doors opened. Once I had shown Jenny what I had brought in with me – flowers and magazines and that kind of thing – we would sit there and chat about the birth, the baby, other patients and anything else that came to mind. Sometimes we would just sit and stare at the bundle of baby I was holding.

We had been told that it was a good idea to restrict the visitors in the evenings, and I must say that it was good

This father spoke for many. The first few days need to be
treasured. Many hospitals do try to keep the evening visiting
restricted to fathers and close relatives; often, children are not
permitted. Valid comparisons can be drawn with weddings. Lots
of people may want an invitation, and some may take offence if
they're not asked to go along. Trying to arrange a visiting rota
might be one of the most difficult tasks you have to perform. Your
wife's tiredness can be a valid and useful reason for putting off
some people. It's easy to forget how strenuous childbirth is when
you see your partner sitting up in bed looking simply wonderful;
don't ask her to do too much and do try to keep some visiting time
for you alone.

COMING HOME

Maybe it's not surprising, but apart from the birth itself this was
the time that numerous fathers picked out as being the most
special. There's a kind of magic in leaving the home as two and
returning as three (or more!) The small rituals, such as taking the
baby from the nurse at the hospital or crossing the threshold of
one's home with the new arrival, can be memorable events.
Unfortunately, just like the first few days in hospital, there can be
additional and unwanted 'rituals' to perform.

66 I made a common mistake which I now regret very much. My
company had given me some time off and I chose to take it when
Joanne was in hospital. I should have waited until she was at
home. So I was able to bring the baby home and then, the next
day, went back to work. I'm sure I missed some of the best days
and also was unable to help much with all the jobs. **99**

What this particular father didn't mention was that his wife had her mother staying with her for a few days to help out; this made the situation much easier. There is no doubt that the first few days can be very important – they can be great fun, and can engender a feeling of great togetherness – but they can also be difficult.

The first anxiety stems from the very presence of a new baby. Are we doing it right, are we going to drop the baby, the baby is crying a lot . . . is it ill? These natural worries can grow unnecessarily large.

> **"** Although we told ourselves beforehand that we wouldn't fuss the baby, we ended up spending almost every minute of the first few days with it. Even when it was asleep and we were having a moment to ourselves we would have to keep checking it to make sure everything was OK. The most common phrase heard in our house, for the first few months as well as the first few days, was: "Go and check the baby." I always responded when my wife asked this. I knew she wouldn't relax until I had, and I also thought that the time I didn't "go and check the baby" would be the one time when it really needed some assistance. **"**

The father's role in the early days at home is often one of emotional support as much as participation in the new tasks. To be able to tell your partner that everything is as it should be and that babies do sleep a lot or cry a lot may be just as important as changing a nappy.

The difficulty of coping with the new arrival may be simplicity itself when compared with the other, frequently mentioned difficulty, that of dealing with a stream of visitors. It seems ungrateful even to suggest that you may not want to see well-wishers at this time, but this may be the situation. You, your partner and your new child have returned from a very emotional period of your lives. You are starting a completely new chapter in your relationship, your living patterns, your finances – everything. It takes time to adjust. Furthermore, you will be wanting to share moments together that will not be repeated and you will be wanting to give your partner as much rest as possible.

“ We found that those couples who already had children tended to keep away, often because one or other of their children had a cold or something and they didn't want to spread the germs, but mostly because they understood the situation. They all phoned, and that was very nice. We could either take the call or offer to call back later. Some friends, however, turned up unexpectedly and seemed to presume that service would be as normal and that we would be able to leap up and get them a cup of tea or whatever. It became very difficult.

The problem was even worse with the family because they all wanted to come and see the new baby, but very few of them seemed to understand just how much work was involved. I spent hours in the kitchen getting them drinks. The star of the proceedings was one of Jan's aunts who came in twice and took charge of everything while Jan sat with the baby. If we could have had her as the only visitor we would have been quite happy. ”

The problem with controlling the situation is just the same as in hospital. You don't want to cause offence, but you do want to salvage some time for yourself. You will need to exercise your best diplomatic skills.

In many cases it will not be possible for the father to be at home during the first few days. In these situations it might be a good idea to try to arrange for somebody else to offer a couple of hours' help each day. Happily there is often a family member who can help out. Close friends and neighbours, particularly if they have had children themselves, can also fulfil this role. It's not essential but it will give the new mother time to talk and to relax – important aspects of the early days. If you are unable to take time off prepare to have your hands full when you do get home from work. Very young babies take a while to sort out the difference between day and night, so you may well find your household as busily active during the night as it is during the day.

It should be pointed out that during the first few days you can expect daily visits from medical staff, either midwives, health visitors or your GP. These are valuable moments for you to discuss any queries you have. You will find, however, that you sometimes just get the baby off to sleep and the doorbell will ring. It is a good idea, if at all possible, to try to fix a time when the visit is going to occur. You will then be able to plan your baby's sleep, bath, feed or whatever. You may also be able to arrange your work duties to allow you to be at home for a couple of these visits. With the pressures on their time, however, it may be difficult for the person to be too precise about when they are going to call.

So far in this section we have talked about fathers in their role as supporting members of the cast; they have been answering phone calls, making coffee and dealing with offended relatives. Naturally, many fathers want to do a lot more than this, and in today's society unemployment, self-employment, shift work, working from home and even house-husbandry do often permit this. But whatever role is chosen, the first few days are important in establishing patterns and habits.

Assuming a hospital birth you will probably find that your wife has been told how to change, bath, feed, burp, dress and undress the baby. You too will need to learn these skills. If you quickly get into the habit of changing the nappy or making up the baby's bedding then you will find there's nothing very complicated about it all. As important as performing the routine chores, however, is being willing and able to make the decisions about what baby wears, when she goes back to her crib or cot, when she needs feeding, whether she is too hot or too cold in what she's wearing, and so on. This area is one that fathers all too often leave entirely to the mother.

❝ I found that I quickly got going on some aspects of bringing up the baby – but that other matters, even now, are still a mystery to me. For example, I could sort out a bath, check that the water was the right temperature, do the "topping and tailing" first and dry and dress it. But I couldn't tell you when it's next due for a feed – or when it had its last one. That's always been my wife's job. **❞**

❝ The difference in our roles is exemplified by the business of going out. I can dress the baby, but my wife chooses the clothes. I'll install the baby in the car seat or pushchair, but my wife will give me the extra blanket or the gloves that she thinks the baby needs. We joke about it, but I'm the menial tasks department and she's the managing director. **"**

Sorting out just how much a father can do is just one side of the story. Many fathers liked to establish just how *little* they were going to do towards bring up their children. This book is written with an underlying faith in the value of shared parenthood – and that means sharing the time-consuming and boring jobs as well as the exciting and stimulating aspects of childrearing. However, you may take comfort from the fact that, if you decide to avoid nappy changing, feeding, dressing etc., you will be in good company and probably in with the majority of fathers. Whichever line you choose, the early days at home will be important for establishing later patterns of involvement and co-operation.

REGISTERING YOUR CHILD

One of the most enjoyable tasks to perform during the early days is to register the child. This frequently ends up as the father's job although it can be very pleasant to go to the registrar's office as a family.

The doctor, midwife or other medical professional involved with your birth will inform the registrar's office via the area health authority that a birth has occurred; they will also inform you of this notification. It is your responsibility to register your child in person. You have forty-two days in which to do this, thus giving you plenty of time to sort out any arguments about the child's name! Should you miss the forty-two-day deadline, just phone the registrar's office and explain. There are simple procedures for registering your child up to one year after the birth; it becomes much more complicated after that. There should be no excuse, because the local registrar's office will send you a reminder after one month.

The normal practice today is to issue a small certificate free of charge; the larger certificates cost a nominal amount. It is worth pointing out that state benefits for the mother and child are often available only after the production of a birth certificate.

OTHER IMPORTANT MATTERS

Your baby represents another life, and one with legal claims and rights. Shortly after the birth of your first child is a good time to think about your will and what might happen to your child should one, other or both of you die. The best advice is to pay a quick visit to your solicitor or the Citizens' Advice Bureau. You can learn more about appointing guardians for your children, wording your will correctly and the ways in which you can insure for your children's future in the case of a death in the family. In the case of unmarried parents you can discuss the implications of a child being born outside marriage.

Naturally these are concerns for both parents, but they frequently fall to the father, usually because he may have a bit less than the mother to think about in the first few days of the baby's life.

WILL I GET ANY SLEEP?

Despite the wonder and beauty of the creation of new life, two rather mundane topics – sleep and nappies – seem to dominate conversations about children in their first year or so. Perhaps the reason why the problem of sleeping patterns receives so much attention is that there is no simple explanation as to why some children sleep a lot more than others – and why some children decide that the day is for sleeping and the night is for being awake! Furthermore, the question of sleep is one of those where somebody else is always having a more successful time than you. You can rest assured that, after a particularly bad night, your friend or neighbour will proudly announce that their little darling was 'going through the night' at six weeks.

Although there are very few generalizations that can be made, it is true to say that children under the age of one year do need a lot of sleep and will probably spend much of their time between feeds sleeping. It's also generally true that children, although they will establish patterns for themselves, can change at any time; the child who goes through the night at six months may be very wakeful at one year, and vice versa.

As with many topics covered in this book there is a lot more to say about sleep than there is room for here. Most large baby-care volumes have entire chapters devoted to sleeping patterns, recommended types of bedding, sleeping postures and so forth. You and your partner might find it useful to read up on this topic, although your medical advisor at the time of the birth will give you some information about the safest way to let your child sleep.

For you, as a first-time father, there are pressing questions about how your baby's sleep (and sleeplessness) may affect your own life. If you are the major, or only, breadwinner in the family then you will understandably be concerned about the effect of sleepless nights on your work. One professional footballer interviewed would book himself into a hotel on the night before a big match so he could be assured of an uninterrupted night's sleep – selfish, or merely practical? Other factors may be important too. For example, how do you cope as parents if you are living in a closely confined flat or shared accommodation? There may be great pressure on you to keep your child quiet at night in order not to disturb others. Also, if you are the kind of person who feels he needs a certain number of hours' sleep, then interrupted nights may well be quite disturbing. Tired parents and tired babies can be the cause of a great deal of stress. It is not selfish or petty to worry about the amount of sleep your child, and therefore you, is getting. Your pattern of sleep and your body's need for it will probably have been developed over a period of twenty years or more. Major interruptions to that pattern are going to cause a disturbance in your general rhythm of life.

What are the sorts of problem that can be anticipated, and are there any ways of overcoming the worst effects of a baby who regularly wakes up at night? The first few months are sometimes the most difficult.

❝ Amy would sleep a lot at first but we knew that she would wake up for a feed in the early hours of the morning. She liked her feed regularly and used to get her last one at night at around ten o'clock. She would sleep soundly until about two or three and then cry for another feed. We had it off to a fine art. Fiona would go and heat up some milk and put the kettle on. I would pick up Amy and soothe her for a few minutes. Then Fiona would return and begin the feeding while I went downstairs to make tea. I would come back and finish off most of the feed; we would always save a drop of milk for after her change of nappy. It was then change, finish feed (and tea) and back to sleep. The whole process took about forty minutes.

This went on for about six months until, slowly, the time became later in the morning and she would wake at about six; we counted that as 'going through the night'. **"**

Amy's parents worked out a regular pattern and, happily, their daughter obligingly seemed to stick to it. Most fathers were able to describe some some kind of structure to the way they dealt with the need to feed during the night. A major determinant was whether the child was being fed by breast or bottle. In the former case it is more difficult for the father to play a fully active role, although of course, tea and sympathy do go a long way.

There are numerous ways that parents develop to cope with interruptions in their night's sleep. Thermos flasks with warm milk, watching pre-recorded soap operas at three in the morning, taking turns to deal with the baby and using the time to catch up on reading were all mentioned. But these methods are responses to a situation where the baby wakes up once or twice in a fairly regular way. Many babies, and many older children, find it difficult to go to sleep and to stay asleep. How does this affect life?

" For the first couple of weeks we expected that Natan would be awake from time to time during the night. Because it was all so new to us I don't think we really noticed that he was asleep during most of the day and awake during most of the night. After the initial period, however, we began to wonder when we would ever get a night's sleep again. Nothing would shift him from the pattern of more sleep during the day than the night. He would cry for a feed and then quite happily sit up and look around him. He was fine unless we tried to put him back in his cot. He would then cry again. We would spend hours, or at least it seemed like hours, walking up and down the room trying to get him off to sleep. But it would only be a shallow kind of sleep and he would soon wake up again.

It soon became rather miserable for us. We didn't enjoy going to bed because sleep was always broken and we always felt we had to be as quiet as possible; the slightest noise apparently woke Natan up. **"**

❝ At night we would get Natalie off to sleep, normally quite happily, at about ten o'clock. She would then sleep until one or two in the morning and want to remain awake until about six. We used to get her back to sleep and then lie in bed, hardly daring to breathe, hoping against hope not to hear that cry. But we knew once she had started we would need to feed her, comfort and rock her and go through a long procedure before she would be ready for even a short **❞** sleep again.

Many other fathers described similar times. The problem of a child that won't sleep at night is compounded by the effect it has on the parents. They become tired and fractious, the baby's behaviour can be resented and a cycle of low morale and mild depression can be established. The baby can sleep during the day to catch up on what has been missed; this is not normally possible for the parents. Two ways of dealing with the problem exist. Either one can modify one's own lifestyle to fit in with that of the baby, or else one can try to change the baby's habits. Needless to say, the latter is the more popular option, but it's also the harder and a certain amount of compromise is often the result.

❝ We actually got around to speaking to the doctor about it. Not because we thought there was a medical problem but because he might have had some magical answer. He did advise keeping the baby awake more during the day. Both Donna and I used to do some work at home and so we always used to take the soft option when Zoe was asleep – we would let her sleep. As a result of the doctor's advice things did get a bit better but it is very hard, when all is peaceful and quiet, to go and wake up a soundly sleeping baby in the knowledge that she will cry and need a great deal of attention.

We just changed our lives a little, in particular not minding if the other went to sleep for ten minutes during the day. I must say that, as much as we loved Zoe, there were times when she was called every name under the sun. This was particularly so in the early hours of the morning when everything always **❞** seems worse anyway.

Apart from trying to induce a change in the baby's pattern of sleep, other remedies that fathers put forward were giving the baby an enormous feed as its last of the day, putting extra bedclothes on once the baby had fallen asleep and leaving a tape recorder playing with some soft background noise (music or spoken word) for the first half-hour or so. The general consensus of advice in this area is to try to find something that works for you – and then stick to it. Babies do seem to find comfort in regular patterns of behaviour. Just as the cycle of sleeplessness and frustration can take you further away from ever finding a solution, so the relaxed and happy parents of a child who sleeps will have more energy and enthusiasm for their child during its daytime waking hours.

If you have a problem with your child's sleep, then changes in your own lifestyle are almost inevitable. The first thing you may find is that, after many years of needing eight hours' sleep, you can suddenly get by with seven. You may find you start going to bed an hour or so earlier, or you may suddenly become an early riser, getting in your household chores at six in the morning because your baby has woken you up and you can't get off to sleep again. Small changes to one's own patterns can make all the difference. What was previously a problem ceases to be one, simply because you have altered your approach.

So far, the discussion has been about how the problems of a wakeful child affect both the parents. Interestingly it was in the area of night-time duties that some of the less selfless male attitudes surfaced. Many fathers claimed that they simply never woke up and so, when it was announced that their little treasure had woken up four times in the night, they looked quite surprised. Other fathers stuck to the gender divide, saying that it was the mother's job to look after the child and so her job to care for the child at night – but before these fathers are dismissed as uncaring and unsharing, they all took an active hand in matters *during the day*. The most common excuse for lack of help in the early hours was that sleeplessness for the father impaired his abilities at work. It is very important that discussion takes place between the parents on the whole question of sleep. It is an area where both parents may have legitimate needs and resentment can soon build up if one or other appears to be unreasonable. The problem may be exacerbated because the moments of crisis occur when neither party is feeling at its best; in such circumstances the child may be the one to suffer.

There is no doubt that sleepless nights cause a lot of difficulty. If you can keep your cool with a screaming child at any time you're doing well – to do so at three in the morning when you're very tired and have a busy day ahead is highly commendable.

Some children come into the world and immediately decide that the best policy is to get in a good ten or twelve hours' sleep every night. You'll be a lucky parent if this happens to you. While it can be claimed that a calm and caring background can help a child feel settled, there is still no doubt that luck plays a big part in matters. This can be confirmed by a common question of doctors and midwives; they often ask new parents whether or not they 'got a sleeper'. Let's hope you get one.

ANXIETY ABOUT SLEEP

If your child sleeps during the day and not at night then you have a problem. If, however, your young child sleeps neither during the day nor at night then he or she may have a problem. In such situations it is obviously advisable to check with your doctor to make sure that there is nothing fundamentally wrong.

Finally, although there is nothing more soothing than watching the gentle rise and fall of your baby's bedding as he or she snores happily away, there will always be a slight element of worry when your child is absolutely quiet. This may sound hard to believe when this section, so far, has dealt with the pain and problems of children who won't sleep. But you will not find many fathers who, in the first few months at least, didn't act the same as this one.

66 The most common phrase around the house was: "Just go and check Julie." As soon as we had got her off to sleep we would have to look in to see that she was OK. Sometimes I would have to touch her in order to see her move, just to make sure she was still alive. As soon as either of us got it into our heads to check her, we had to go and do it; the thought was always there, in the back of our minds, that the one time we didn't check her would be the one time that she needed some assistance. 99

Perhaps associated with this general concern was a more specific anxiety about the babies who die in so-called 'cot deaths'. There is only a tiny number of such deaths each year, and such is the lack of knowledge about the problem that it's not even clear that all the deaths are from the same cause. In this state of ignorance there is little you can do in preventative terms apart from taking all the recognized precautions for a child's normal sleep. Don't worry is the best advice, and don't feel silly if you feel the need to look in on your son or daughter every twenty minutes or so. As one father explained:

66 The very best moments were when Jackie and I would go and stand over Jack's cot while he was asleep. He would often be quietly snoring and occasionally twitching his face, completely unaware that two grown adults were watching him with lumps in their throats and tears in their eyes. 99

WHAT IF MY BABY CRIES A LOT?

Crying is the one way a young baby has of communicating with its parents. Seen like this it can be both a helpful indicator of requirements and the first step towards building a relationship. Crying, however, can also be very noisy, very irritating and often quite inexplicable. The mere fact that a baby apparently has all it needs is not enough to guarantee that it won't cry.

Crying, like sleeping, is frequently taken to be an indication of whether or not you have a 'good' baby. Of course, we all know what people mean when they ask us if our child is 'good', but it can be hurtful to think that we have a 'bad' baby just because it cries a lot. The baby is not being bad, he or she is simply making life difficult for us.

WHY BABIES CRY

Knowing why babies cry doesn't mean you can always stop them. Generally, however, it's a good start. Babies tend to cry if they are hungry, uncomfortable, anxious or ill. Being uncomfortable may be the result of having a dirty nappy, being too cold or too hot, needing winding, or even simple things like lying on a toy in their cot or being in a draught. Anxiety can be a response to the mood of the parents or simply an expression of unhappiness at feeling ignored or lonely. Illness is less easy to spot, but should a baby cry

125

continually, and especially if the crying is accompanied by very clammy skin and wriggling or writhing, it's best to seek proper medical advice.

> 66 Our experience was that our baby was very sensitive to what was going on around him. He would cry quite readily when anything disturbed his cosy world and would also cry if he could detect odd changes in mood. For example, he would always let rip if Jane and I shouted at one another, and once burst into a long wail when gunfire and shouts on the television upset him. Fortunately, he was quite easily shut up too. 99

> 66 Ours tended not to cry much when hungry, but always got into a state near to bedtime. She would be very tired and couldn't get to sleep. Sometimes we had to leave her to cry herself off to sleep because she would not be comforted. 99

The good news, or in some cases bad news, is that habits in crying can change just as readily as habits in, say, sleeping. A 'crier' can turn out to be quiet at the age of two or three – and vice versa.

A QUESTION OF PATIENCE

Knowing the likely cause of crying means you will know what the baby needs. You provide it, and the baby stops crying. If only it were so easy. In many situations, of course, the simple solution does solve the problem. Unfortunately, there are many times when a baby will go on crying uncontrollably. The baby's cry, especially if heard in the middle of the night, can be the signal for a lot of wasted time, lost sleep and negative emotions. In very blunt terms, if babies didn't cry there would be far fewer cases of adults harming their children in fits of rage and frustration.

> 66 I got very miserable at times, going to bed, getting warm and sleepy, and knowing that I would soon be hearing Robert's

little wail. Most nights I would get off to sleep and it would come into my dreams. If it was "my turn" I would get up, pick him up and take him downstairs to fix his drink. Making up his bottle would take seven or eight minutes, during which time he would cry continually. Comforting him could get him quiet, but only for a few moments. He really wanted his drink and so it was normally best to press ahead with it as quickly as possible, leaving him to scream – which he did very loudly.

His drink would quieten him and we would sit for a while as he drank it, was burped and changed. A last drop of milk, and the struggle to get him off to sleep began again. It was as if his cry was just beneath the surface all the while. He would look sleepy, close his eyes and even start to snore but somehow would produce a cry. This would set him off and it would take another ten to twenty minutes to get him settled again. It was just the same during the day; any periods of quiet were so fragile, you knew that he might start crying at any minute. It put a great strain on us for almost two years. **"**

For this father, and for numerous others, it was simply a question of patience. Getting a baby to stop crying can take an age. Often it's the kind of job that you can't combine with much else. Trying to read, or cook, or type is all very difficult. Watching television or listening to the radio are often the only options – assuming you're not talking to your child, of course.

Sensing that a crying baby wastes a lot of time can create a lack of patience and a tenseness or anger that is normally counter-productive.

" It took me only a short while to realize that patience is the key. On more than one occasion I was so angry with Zoe for her continual sobbing that I stuffed her back in her cot, shouted loudly at her and stormed off out of the room. This only made her scream all the louder. Getting angry can never be the solution for the baby; it only makes them worse. **"**

It's easy to recommend being calm and patient, but hard, in

reality, to achieve. A baby's cry does 'go right through you'. When a baby is crying its face is contorted and its whole demeanour is aggressive and taut. It's surely harder to love a crying and kicking baby than one that is cooing and gently waving its hands. So what can be done?

❝ We found the key was to share, so at least only one of us had the problem. "It's your turn" became a familiar household phrase. The partner not trying to stop the baby crying had to feel conscience-free and press on with whatever he or she was doing. It would be their turn pretty soon. ❞

❝ Taking the baby over when it was crying was, I'm sure, one of the best things I did for Amanda. When things got too much she would just shove the baby at me and go off for ten minutes. It just took the pressure off. ❞

SOME REMEDIES

It's likely that a father will spend less time with the baby than the mother and therefore have less excuse for feeling that the crying is all getting too much. He can help his partner out by understanding just how frustrating a continually crying baby can be, and he can also suggest or try out some of the more commonly recommended methods of stopping the baby's inexplicable crying.

Movement is often thought to be the best remedy. It can be the gentle rocking of the baby in its parent's arms, the motion of a pram or car, or being carried along in one of the front or back child carriers. At least you can be getting exercise yourself with some of these ideas.

A dummy is another favourite method of getting baby to stop crying. It doesn't always work and does have its critics. The main objection lies in the dependence that might be created. This really is an individual's decision, although on purely medical grounds it is worth warning against using a sweetened dummy. This can lead only to an unhealthy desire for sweet things and a lot of tooth decay and gum problems.

In extreme situations some parents resort to using a proprietary brand of baby medicine. Small amounts can be mixed with the baby's drink. It helps to soothe the baby and aid sleep and is recommended when the child is suffering from a cold or some other simple complaint. The instructions should be read carefully and these liquids should not be used as nightly sleeping pills.

The last suggestion is the much favoured 'five-minute' rule – adapted by some parents to become the ten-minute or even twenty-minute rule. You first check that you have gone through the normal list of things that might make a baby cry. Then, assuming you have ensured that it is fed, changed, warm and dry, and if you have tried your other techniques of soothing, you simply leave it. The important point is to set a pre-determined amount of time. For example, you start with five minutes. You walk away from the baby and don't come back until five minutes have passed. During those minutes you do whatever you want, taking care to drown out the baby with noise of your own. Amazingly, this works more often than not; it also helps the baby to start to spend time without the constant administerings of one or other parent.

> **“** We aimed to share Gary's upbringing as much as possible, but it tended to be Gail's job a lot more than mine. She got very upset when Gary cried a lot, which he did, during the first few months. The midwife had suggested leaving him to cry for a while but Gail didn't like to do it. So, once or twice when I was left with Gary, I experimented. I left him screaming on one occasion, while I listened outside the door. Quickly he shut up. I crept in and he was wide awake but making no noise at all. Another time I crept back in and he saw me – and started screaming again! My theory was that he didn't cry when he thought nobody could hear him. I eventually got Gail to try the idea and it worked for her too. Now that Gary is about five months he regularly gets periods on his own – crying or not – and I think it does us all good. **”**

This section couldn't be allowed to pass without a word from the father whose daughter had a tracheotomy (hole in the throat where the normal breathing channels are restricted).

" We went to Great Ormond Street for the third time, when she was about two years old, to see if the tube could, at last, come out. They took her into the operating theatre, found everything was OK, and took out the tube. She started breathing through her mouth instead of her throat and, almost immediately, started bawling with those hitherto unused vocal chords. It was magic. **"**

WHAT IS POST-NATAL DEPRESSION?

You may have been surprised by some of your partner's activities during the pregnancy, especially if she experienced cravings or went on a nest-building spree. It's likely also that some aspects of her character, perhaps her expressive language, will have caused a few raised eyebrows during the labour and birth. The surprises, however, do not stop there. The early days and weeks after the birth can be very difficult for the new mother and, as a result, for the new father too.

Most women are likely to feel a little low a few days after the birth. It's suggested that this is just a reaction to all the emotional highs of the preceding days, or possibly a realization that having a baby is a life-changing event, with all that that implies. Whatever the cause, these 'blues', as they are known, soon pass as the body and mind return to a state of equilibrium, and as both partners instinctively accept the vital task of looking after the baby. That the 'blues' soon pass does not mean that the father can't help the process by giving that bit more support and understanding; the important point is that there is nothing to worry about.

Post-natal depression, however, is very different from this short-lived and entirely expected condition. This kind of depression will be a long-term condition for the woman where she cannot rid herself of feelings of sadness, inadequacy and even helplessness. She will find that the baby is all too much for her; she wakes up and goes to sleep feeling depressed and loses the drive to take up new challenges or to return to activities she enjoyed before the birth.

66 The frustrating facet of Kathleen's post-natal depression was how aware she was of it. So we could talk about it, even tell other people about it, and yet seemingly fail to conquer it. Seeing people and being jolly was a struggle for Kathleen but she managed it so well that many of our friends had no idea that anything was wrong. Unfortunately, the effort of will-power required to appear cheerful for a short while used to leave Kathleen extra tired and weepy afterwards.

Of course, there were some people we met who thought it was all a mythical disease and that Kathleen was just being neurotic. If only they knew. **99**

This father's last statement implies a very difficult situation behind the closed doors of home. Fathers can feel the pressure intensely. The problems of bringing up a new baby are compounded by having a partner in a very unstable emotional condition. Father has to take much more responsibility but has to tread carefully to avoid adding to his partner's sense of inadequacy. Arguments and recriminations are very likely as two tired people struggle with one partner's illness and the combined need to project a loving and happy emotional front to the new child.

True post-natal depression needs proper medical care. A doctor will talk to you about the problem and may, often as a last resort, prescribe drugs to help your partner with some of the immediate symptoms.

There is no hard and fast dividing line between the 'blues' and post-natal depression. The advice for coping with either condition is similar. Fathers can help a great deal, of course, by talking, understanding and offering practical help. Assuming you are already taking your share of the chores, the most commonly heard recommendation is to let your partner go out by herself. And if she doesn't want to, try to persuade her.

66 I have to confess that I used to encourage Penny to go out, but didn't really want her to do it. I wasn't too keen on looking after the baby by myself. When, after a particularly unhappy day, she phoned up a friend and agreed to go out for a drink, I couldn't go back on my offer. However, once she was gone I enjoyed it immensely. I was in charge and was able to look after Petra all by myself.

Since then I've grown in confidence and Penny goes out much more frequently. Also, now Petra is old enough to leave with baby-sitters and so we can go out togther more often. **"**

Going out means being away from the baby, but it will also be a chance for your partner to be herself and not just a mother of somebody else. If you listen to conversations and greetings, mothers do cease to be people in their own right and end up as just 'Johnny's mother' instead. To aid this progression, a gift for your partner in her role of woman rather than mother may be most welcome.

Dealing with any problems of post-natal depression or the 'blues' can be so much commonsense. Being aware is the key, and knowing your partner is the start of the solution. Two books worth recommending are *Towards Happy Motherhood: Understanding Post-Natal Depression* by Maggie Comport (Corgi) and *Depression after Childbirth* by Katharina Dalton (Oxford University Press). They both touch on the role of the father/partner.

DO MEN SUFFER POST-NATAL DEPRESSION?

Fathers do not suffer from true post-natal depression. Many fathers, however, go through a period of unhappiness and uncertainty shortly after the birth of their first child. Some reasons for this, such as failing to establish a relationship with the new child, feeling the pressure on the relationship with the partner and generally being tired, are all touched upon elsewhere in the book. But there are other reasons for the depression, all linked in some way to the major change in life that is experienced.

Perhaps the most important factor is to accept the depression as a normal occurrence that can be discussed openly. Men are frequently bad at expressing their emotions, and at the time of the birth this trait will be worsened by the fact that everybody is expecting them to be overjoyed, not depressed. The situation is not unlike others that touch upon emotional affairs, namely that many other people share your experience but few want to talk about it. There may be that sense of guilt attached to a bout of post-natal blues, or even the fear that something is wrong with you. Don't worry.

> **❝** I think the arguing with Janine was the hardest thing to accept. We had never fallen out before and suddenly were bickering on a daily basis. She said I was very grumpy and difficult to live with – and she was right. I thought of all the things that were making me miserable, such as lack of money, lack of sleep, lack of social life, but really couldn't put it down to any one of them. I had expected to experience a big change, and here it was. The problem, I think, was that so many negative things happened at once. And in the early days at least, I didn't seem to be getting much in return from our new baby. **❞**

Listing some of the things that often have to go by the board, temporarily at least, can be a sobering exercise. Perhaps it's no wonder that fathers get depressed; the change in life, however well anticipated, is a major one.

The suggestions for dealing with depression in new mothers mostly involved the father taking some positive and supportive action. Unfortunately, it's unrealistic to expect a new mother to be able to lend much support to her partner, apart from helping him talk about the problem.

> **❝** I found I couldn't really talk about my feelings because people would have just thought me selfish. It would have been selfish to have involved Barbara too. So I kept it bottled up although I was noticeably down at the mouth most of the time.
> As the baby grew and became more responsive I found I was getting more cheerful. I don't say there was necessarily a connection between the two events, but by the time Alan was six months old I was back to my old self and actually talking about having a second child! **❞**

Time seemed to be the great healer in cases of depressed fathers. Since the child is also developing as time passes, it's not unreasonable to suggest a connection between the two. Do fathers generally feel happier about their new role as the child grows? One father applied this bit of amateur psychology to his situation.

❝ Amanda went straight into loving the child. She would coo over it, spend hours talking to it and was really very happy indeed with every aspect of the new arrival. I was not quite the same and actually was very fed up during the first four months or so. But as Chrissie started smiling and chatting (not literally) I took a much greater interest. As soon as my efforts were rewarded with a laugh or a smile I was prepared to put more into it. It grew from there.

I reckon that women are better at showing and giving love than men. I was more selfish, only giving when I was getting something back. If we have another I'm going to try harder to be less selfish in the early weeks and months and hopefully feel better about the whole thing as a result. **❞**

Whether or not the method works, time will tell. But for this father, as for some of the others who struggled a bit in the early days, matters improved as time went by. The key things to remember are that you are not unique in feeling low when you think you should be feeling high, and that your child, for quite a while, will not take too much notice of your mood. Give him or her a bottle and they'll love you forever!

WHAT ARE THE EXTRA JOBS, AND WHY DO THEY CAUSE SUCH PROBLEMS?

The concept of shared parenthood can mean a lot of things. Ensuring the right atmosphere in which your child can express its creativity, providing the right blend of material goods to aid development, and giving the necessary love and comfort to promote health and happiness are all essential tasks for both parents. Equally essential, however, are changing nappies, wiping up sick, providing feeds in the middle of the night and undertaking a seemingly endless stream of washing and ironing. The two types of activity, the emotional support and the practical tasks, are inextricably mixed. A child will not feel very creative if it's hungry, nor will it be happy or healthy with a dirty nappy and unhygienic surroundings.

It's worth looking, briefly, at the practical tasks because they underpin the whole business of child-rearing. Without them the child cannot flourish, and in their absence it's pointless to attempt a proper nurturing of the child's capabilities. And although they are only fairly menial jobs, they are frequently the cause of great friction between the mother and father, and of great uncertainty and concern for fathers-to-be.

“ I kept insisting that, as much as possible, we would share the jobs when the baby arrived. My friends who were fathers tended to keep quiet about this proposal, while mothers looked questioningly at me and admiringly at my wife. Little did I know what I was letting myself in for.

Rather than try to do things together we decided, for better or for worse, that there would be times when I would take over completely from my wife. The couple of hours from five until seven in the evenings were mine and two or three hours on Saturday and Sunday mornings. This isn't to say that I didn't do anything else in the rest of the time, but that during these periods I did everything.

I was kept constantly busy because these were periods when the baby was awake. The evening sessions entailed a bath and a last drink before bed, while the morning periods were when the baby needed feeding, changing and playing with. There never seemed to be a minute spare; Andrew cried if he was left alone. I had to abandon plans to do anything else, devoting the time entirely to being a father.

Two problems ensued. The first was that I had my time with baby in some of my only free time from work – so when I wasn't working . . . I was working! I knew that my wife needed the support, but I was having to give it when I felt like it least. The second difficulty was a result of me doing things differently from my wife. She would frequently tell me how I was doing things wrong, or worse, she would come and take over for a few minutes. Quite frankly I didn't enjoy the time spent with young Andrew. I was nearly always relieved when he went to bed; sometimes he got very short change from me I'm afraid. **"**

This quote is included particularly as an indication of how the pressure of the necessary chores can undermine the best-intentioned parents. This couple decided to divide up the tasks into set periods. Some choose to work on a much more ad hoc basis, while others again divide jobs up so the mother does most of the feeding, the father does the baths and so on. The way jobs are divided must be a shared decision, the major determining factor probably being the way the household is run generally. For example, is the mother going to be at home most of the time, does father have flexible working hours or is the father going to become a house-husband? However the sharing is done, the jobs still remain.

A LOT OF POO AND SICK

This sub-heading was chosen as it was one father's considered view of what bringing up a young child meant. There's no escaping the unpleasantness of certain human functions, and fathers' conversation often seems to display a fascination with them. Give a new father a drink, start talking about nappies, and you are likely as not going to get a graphic lecture on just what a tiny baby can produce. There's not much point in saying a great deal about changing nappies except to point out that a slick father, using disposable nappies or not, can normally accomplish the whole procedure in three minutes or less; it's quite a small price to pay for your child's comfort and health.

In the first six months of life a baby may need a nappy change about six times a day. It gets less as the child gets older, and many parents like to leave children without nappies if they are outdoors in the summer. Most children establish a routine fairly quickly so you will soon know when it's a good time to change and a good time to wait. Mopping up other mess is similarly simple and quick, especially if you are prepared with a bowl and a cloth at the ready.

Feeding is perhaps next on the list of jobs that fathers like talking about. Once your child is no longer feeding from the breast, and sometimes before if you fill bottles with mother's milk, feeding becomes a major consumer of time. Apart from the actual process of holding a bottle in your child's mouth, there's the making up of powdered milks, heating (and inevitable cooling down because you've overheated), washing and sterilizing to be done. After a bottle feed the baby needs winding too. Again, there's nothing very mystical about the job, but it does take up a lot of time.

❝ I used to compare feeding with sitting in a wheelchair. I felt so helpless, perched there watching the world go on around me. It really irritated me because there seemed to be very little else I could do. It wasn't really a very good time to try to form a relationship with our baby either because all she wanted to do was drink. Eventually I used to arrange it so I could sit down in front of the television and accept feeding time as a rest period for me; but doing it five times a day, admittedly only at weekends, became very boring. **"**

The process of getting baby off to sleep is sometimes coupled with feeding. Many babies, like their adult counterparts, can sleep at any time, anywhere. Others, however, do take a lot of persuading, commonly done by walking the baby up and down whilst whispering sweet nothings in its ear. Surely that's a pleasant chore? Not when your dinner's getting cold, you're due to go out to the cinema and you've already spent an hour at it. As with feeding, some fathers experienced the 'wheelchair' feeling and it caused resentment and frustration at times.

Dressing and undressing baby is another relatively simple but time-consuming chore. Accidents with nappies, spilt milk or just natural dribbling often necessitate extra changes of clothes. A new baby needs to be kept warm and may be wearing several layers on cold days. All this means not only time spent changing but also hours washing and ironing.

In addition to those jobs that are essential to baby you will find that some of your own actions are slowed down because of baby's presence. The main example is going out of the house. This will normally entail extra clothes for the baby, setting up a car seat or pram and, if you are going to be away for more than a couple of hours, packing a bag of emergency baby items.

The main problem with the jobs that are associated with baby should, by now, be apparent. Individually the tasks don't present any great difficulty, but together they constitute a formidable timetable of duties. The sheer number of them is quite daunting and can be very tiring. Take a couple of tired parents, mix in a screaming baby, and there's the recipe for friction and discord. One other problem can also result.

" We seemed to spend so much time doing jobs for James that we were either too tired or too busy to take time just to talk to and pamper him. I felt this quite keenly because I had held this vision of forming a strong bond between myself and my child. This, I thought, would result from hours spent playing or just being together in his early life. Instead, I spent most of my time wiping his face with a flannel or his bottom with a "baby wipe". He's now three and a half and I don't think it's done him any harm at all, but at the time I was worried. I had wanted to find time for a "father's hour" each day but was so relieved when he went to bed at night that I quickly reduced that ambition to spending a few moments each morning with him after his first feed of the day. **"**

Several fathers hinted at guilt feelings in this respect. They had wanted to spend quiet and reflective moments with their children but their good intentions were lost in the welter of jobs to be done. At times when the baby was not needing attention they would fit in some personal time, perhaps catching up on household chores or just taking the opportunity to read the paper or have a cup of tea.

CAN THE SITUATION BE IMPROVED?

Apart from hiring help there's no way to avoid doing the necessary tasks. Many fathers, of course, simply don't do many, or any, of the jobs mentioned above, happily seeing them as women's work or explaining away their apparent idleness as part of the division of labour in their household. But for those parents actively pursuing the goal of shared parenthood the situation need not be too bleak. Tiredness, arguments and a neglected baby are not necessarily the result of the extra hours of work that a baby entails. Organization was the key for many.

> **"** Simply putting everything away where it belonged saved hours and hours. It sounds like a silly point to make, but with young children you really need to be organized. Minor emergencies were happening all the time, like Gemma being sick or managing to soil her clothes as well as her nappy. For everybody's sake it was best to get things cleared up as quickly as possible. This meant knowing where the floor cloth, the disinfectant, the clean nappies, the change of clothes etc. were kept.
>
> There's nothing more stressful than trying to find things while your baby is screaming at you from one room and your wife, who has left you in charge, is demanding to know what's wrong from another. **"**

What this father forgot to add about this predicament is that it is the one time that the phone is almost guaranteed to ring.

Being organized can only make the jobs easier; it cannot resolve the problem of trying to fit a completely new batch of responsibilities into a day that was probably already full. Planning how you are going to manage this feat may be like your financial predictions: it may not seem possible, but somehow you know that you will manage.

> **"** Caroline and I actually sat down to discuss it because it was getting on top of us. We found we really couldn't cope with everything that needed doing – and we were thinking about

having more than one child! In the end we looked at the complete array of things that needed doing and started to cut out some of them. Most of the jobs for the baby had to remain but we ironed fewer clothes, bought more convenience foods, dusted, cleaned and tidied up less regularly. This was the only way we could absorb the extra jobs and still keep some time for ourselves. This last point was important to us as we had seen too many friends become what we called "professional" parents, losing their own identity in the daily effort to get everything right for precious baby.

As a result of this our house was not so clean or tidy as before. We didn't do any decorating for a long time and the garden was neglected badly too. Generally, and importantly, we kept our heads when many (not all) around seemed to be losing theirs. 99

To go on much more would be to present an unduly depressing picture of the work required to bring up a baby. By now you should have the general impression that it's not that easy. Attitude, however, may be the key to the situation. If you can come to terms with living in a less than tidy house and sleeping in unironed sheets, you may also be able to accept that washing out soiled nappies is fun and walking up and down with a crying baby is life-enhancing. Importantly, a changed attitude to unpleasant chores may help your relationship with your child to grow.

66 I resented the fact that I spent so much time doing basically horrible jobs. I also was unhappy that our baby seemed to be all work and very little pleasure. On the advice of a friend, however, I tried to treat the jobs as more fun and more of a co-operative effort between Jack [the baby] and me. I would always talk to him as I worked and tried to encourage him to play with the bottles and tubes required for bathing, changing or feeding him. I used the time spent on jobs as my time with him, hoping it would help us to get to know one another.

It didn't always work and sometimes I still got fed up and frustrated. Generally, however, I was much happier with Jack and in myself. 99

HOW CAN WE PROTECT OUR PATTERN OF LIFE?

We saw earlier that the birth of a new baby can occasion radical changes in the parents' social life. It is quite likely that you will spend less time and money on going out, and that you will find yourself socializing more with other parents than with childless couples or individuals.

Whether or not these changes occur, and whether or not they surprise you, may depend on your ante-natal preparations and expectations. Most parents know that life will be different after the birth but few really want to accept this fact. This kind of thinking leads to the 'I'm not going to let it change my life' attitude. Of the parents who boast this, some are quite serious and do try to carry on as if nothing, or at least very little, has changed.

Of course, for many fathers the birth need not herald a new regime. Regular and long-distance commuters, those who work away from home for long stretches, and those who refuse to take an active part in the child-rearing process, can all continue their former lives with very little interruption. But what about the fathers (and mothers) who want or need to be involved, are happy and able to accept their responsibilities and yet wish to carry on as much as possible as before? Is there a way to enjoy the best of both worlds?

GOING OUT OR ENTERTAINING AT HOME

Home can quickly become the centre for one's new social life. The reason is that home contains baby's bed, bottles and changing equipment. These are all transportable items, but it's much easier if they stay in one place.

> 66 To be perfectly honest I was not keen to have children, and much discussion took place before I was convinced it was a good idea. One of the main points I made was that our social life would be ruined. My wife assured me that we would carry on regardless and not let the child dictate to us. Because of this assertion I think we tried too hard to play down the impact of children.
>
> We accepted invitations to go out from very soon after Joe's birth, always checking first that it would be OK if we took Joe along with us. Nobody baulked at the suggestion but, looking back, I wonder if some friends were just being polite and really wanted to say no to Joe. Anyway, we would pack up all the necessary equipment, do our best to keep Joe awake for long periods before the time of departure and hope that he would remain asleep whilst we were eating dinner or enjoying the party. The first few times went well but we ran into a major problem on an evening out with some friends of friends. Joe was sickening for something and would not, or could not, sleep. The meal was a constant series of interruptions as Melanie or I would get up and try to comfort him. Unfortunately his illness and the strange surroundings were too much and we left as soon as possible after the meal. All very embarrassing. The same thing happened again a few weeks later and we began to feel differently about taking Joe with us.
>
> The people we were visiting were great about it, but we felt uncomfortable. As a result of this evening we began to refuse a few more invitations or, when asked out, used to reply by inviting the people over to our home. At our place we felt much happier – and so did Joe. If he was awake he could come down for ten minutes and we could delay the serving of the meal. 99

> 66 I think we were happier about entertaining at home because we always felt self-conscious about taking so much stuff out

with us. Our hosts would open the door to find us standing there with the baby, bedding, a carrycot, nappies, bottles and, somewhere hidden amongst everything else, a gift for the host. It looked as if we were coming for the week! Also, we felt very guilty about our baby disrupting somebody else's plans. Without exception our friends would dismiss any inconvenience as unimportant, but we couldn't help feeling bad about it. Unfortunately we could remember how intolerant we were when we didn't have children – not to their faces, but once they had left. **99**

Whilst the convenience of home very often makes it the centre of the new family's activities, it may be the one place that you, and more particularly your partner, are desperate to get out for a while. Post-natal blues can be accentuated by the feeling of being trapped – going out can be the cure.

Whichever way you decide to approach the problem – going out or staying at home – you will probably depend to a certain extent on the goodwill and understanding of your family and friends. As noted above, it may be impossible to reassure you that the interrupted dinner party or the spilt baby's milk *really* didn't matter at all. It's for reasons like these that you may find that the pattern of your social life changes. Some friends get weeded out of your invitation lists, and you find yourselves cut off by others.

Assuming, however, that you are going to persevere with taking your child around with you as much as possible, are there practical points to remember? The answer is, like so much else in bringing up children, to combine a little thought with a little common sense. For example, if your child goes to sleep at half-past seven then suggest to your hosts that you turn up a few minutes early to settle him or her. If your partner is breast-feeding and you think this may upset other guests (surprisingly common), try to arrange feeds before and after the meal or main event. If you are going to visit people with children, check first to see if they have bedding or a cot you can utilize (with this situation roles can be reversed if people bring their children when visiting you).

Finally in this section, it's worth mentioning that some fathers found that they did most of their entertaining on Sunday afternoons. This meant less bother with the children since they weren't expected to sleep. Furthermore, it was a time when the fathers could help more, either getting the children ready or preparing food and drinks.

LEAVING CHILDREN BEHIND

Much of what has been said above relates to very young children when the parents might be reluctant to leave them with anybody else. Deciding when you can safely and confidently leave children behind must be a personal decision. The controlling factors will probably be the behavioural patterns of the child and the trust you can place in the baby-sitter. Related to these may also be your own sense of anxiety or confidence.

It's when dealing with the question of baby-sitters that the role of the family can be very important. Having mother just around the corner can be a great blessing, and couples who can depend on regular family baby-sitters are very lucky indeed. For those who cannot rely on the services (normally unpaid) of a member of the family, then a baby-sitting circle may be the answer. To many fathers, certainly prior to their child's birth, a baby-sitting circle represents the worst aspects of cosy suburban respectability – only the mid-life crisis left to look forward to! But, like dishwashers, washing machines and other prosaic symbols of the modern world, baby-sitting circles are very practical and useful. Furthermore, they are made of people like you. Numerous fathers were happy to extol the virtues of joining a baby-sitting circle, mostly because it meant they could go out more regularly without extra cost, but in some cases because it gave them a night out when they could work or read untroubled by their own household chores and worries.

> ❝ We waited until Claire was about six months before using the baby-sitting circle. I was quite happy to do so but Pauline worried that Claire would wake up and give the baby-sitter problems. What we ignored was the fact that the circle was run by parents, nearly all of whom were more experienced than us. They knew how to handle a crying baby. On the one occasion that Claire did wake she was, apparently, no trouble at all. In fact we had much worse times when we went out to sit – and that never bothered us. ❞

You can carry on a full social life after the arrival of your child although, like most things, it will just take a little more effort. You will always have your child in the back of your mind – if he's asleep upstairs you will be dreading the sound of crying, and if you've left him at home you will be certain each time the phone rings that it's your baby-sitter.

It's probably wrong to consider looking after baby as a problem, but there are some longer-term 'solutions' such as au pairs or nannies that are considered in the next section of the book. The reason they are not dealt with here is that, generally, parents don't like to hand over the greater proportion of their responsibilities when their child is very young. A child develops very quickly, however, in its early life and can make the move from helpless bundle to fairly sturdy baby in a surprisingly short time. Three months seemed, most commonly, to be the age after which confidence in the baby's health grew and parents felt more ready to use paid help. The options and pitfalls of this are discussed on pages 190–193.

HOW WILL THE BIRTH AFFECT OUR LOVE LIFE?

THE DOCTOR'S CONCERN

You may be surprised to hear one of your doctor's first questions after the birth of your child. He or she will ask your partner what she proposes to do about contraception. Although you and your partner may well be feeling very close at the time, actually making love may be far from your thoughts. The point of the doctor's question is unrelated to desire; it's simply a recognition of the fact that a woman can conceive just as readily after the birth of her child as at any time. And it's at highly emotional periods such as immediately after a birth that precautions can easily be forgotten. What the doctor's question also tells us is that love-making is possible very soon after childbirth.

The woman, in a normal pregnancy and birth, obviously experiences a great physical upheaval. How quickly she recovers depends upon how her body responded to the birth and the degree of rest possible afterwards. She may have had an episiotomy, in which case the stitches will need time to heal, or she may have delivered by Caesarean section which will probably necessitate an even longer recovery time.

Physical recovery is, of course, only part of the story. There are other important factors to consider, foremost amongst them being the emotional effect of the birth on the bond between the father and his partner.

> **“** Claire is an extremely thoughtful and caring person but sometimes this aspect of her nature creates problems for her. For example, I know that she had felt a little guilty about us not making love for several months before George's birth. Our abstinence was due to her general sickness and tiredness during most of the pregnancy. She would sometimes suggest love-making even though it was clear that she didn't really fancy the idea much. I would always tell her it didn't matter . . . whereupon she would confess that she didn't really feel up to it anyway.
>
> After the birth, however, she was quick to raise the subject and suggested that "normal service should be resumed". I smiled at this. It really didn't matter to me, although I was not averse to the idea, especially if Claire was keen. I just sensed that she felt she had to get back to love-making quickly for my sake.
>
> In the event we made love some seven or eight days after George's birth, just a couple of days after Claire left hospital. Perhaps I should have been more patient but I saw no reason to resist the opportunity. Unfortunately, it was pretty disastrous. It was clearly an ordeal for Claire, mostly because of physical discomfort but also, I think, because she just didn't feel right. In fact, after that first session we didn't make love again for almost two months. That was fine, and has been ever since. We should have waited. **”**

NOT JUST A PHYSICAL PROBLEM

Physical discomfort aside, there are many other reasons why resuming former patterns of sexual behaviour might be difficult. Important among these may be your partner's attitude to her own body. Some women feel unhappy about their bodies during their pregnancy, and some experience similar emotions after the birth. The body does not return to normal immediately. There will be a period when the belly is still larger than normal and covered by rather loose flesh; this, quite clearly, is only what is to be expected. Your partner may also have put on extra weight during the pregnancy; this may take some time, and effort, to lose again. These, and other reasons, can often contribute to a sense of disappointment and embarrassment. The disappointment may be felt quite keenly if you and your partner have been looking forward to 'getting back to normal' after the birth.

> **❝** I can honestly say that my wife's appearance didn't matter to me at all. To me she was still the same, even if she was a couple of stones heavier than when she had first become pregnant. But I knew it bothered her. It wasn't so much the weight, but other little things. In particular she used to get unhappy about her breasts. She was breast-feeding and, whenever we made love, they would leak milk. She either had to put up with this or wear a large and unattractive nursing bra. It bothered her a lot. **❞**

More long-lasting than the effects of breast-feeding can be stretch marks. These occur on the skin around the belly. They can take many years to disappear and, in some cases, their impression can be left on the skin permanently.

> **❝** It was definitely the stretch marks that caused us a problem. Jenny had very bad lines criss-crossing her stomach. This was despite taking the recommended precautions during the pregnancy. She felt very unhappy about them, and to this day I don't think anyone has seen them apart from myself and a couple of doctors. She always wears a one-piece bathing costume now instead of going topless or wearing a bikini as she used to.
> When it came to love-making she was very reluctant to do anything unless the lights were off or we were covered by bedclothes. The situation has improved a lot since then but we don't behave like we used to. This may be because of our age and getting used to one another, but I do blame the birth, and in particular the stretch marks, for some of it. **❞**

The 'recommended precautions' that are mentioned by this father mostly consist of simple exercises and rubbing ointment into the body. There is no guarantee that such methods will prevent stretch marks.

Stretch marks, along with all the other possible physical results of childbirth, can clearly affect the woman's attitude to her body and, either directly or indirectly, can influence her approach to love-making. To say that patience and understanding are required from the man is to state the obvious. In practical terms there is little that can be done apart from taking an active interest in any steps to recovery that have been suggested. Just as couples have their own ways of arousing one another for love-making, so personal means will be discovered for bringing the sexual part of a relationship back to normal.

To suggest that the woman's attitude is the only hurdle in the way of relaxed and fulfilling love-making is wrong. Many fathers find problems of their own. One of the most common causes of an inability to enjoy sex shortly after childbirth is that the man has, for the first time, seen the woman 'down there'. It may be surprising for some people to learn that for many men sexual relationships have never been completely unbridled; they are not familiar with their partner's anatomy and are certainly not pre-pared for the raw exposure of a woman that is commonplace during childbirth. The couple of fathers who alluded to this kind of problem explained that they felt unprepared for what was going to happen and, afterwards, thought they would be hurting their partner if they were to make love.

The business of intimacy and exposure actually works both ways. It's not unheard of for the woman to be a little uncertain of herself after childbirth because the man has 'seen everything' and can't, surely, still find her attractive. Comparisons may not be terribly helpful but, in an effort to make her husband understand how she felt, one mother asked him if he would like his genitals to swell up agonizingly to four or five times their normal size before a baby was squeezed out; and all this happening with a handful of people watching very closely. It makes you think.

MALE JEALOUSY

Male jealousy is something that you may have heard about whilst preparing to become a parent. The emotion can affect fathers soon after the birth of their child. Interestingly it was not mentioned by any of the inverviewees for this book, even those who were asked directly about it and who had been open and expansive on other topics.

The basis for the condition is easy to understand. The father finds that, after the birth of his child, his partner's attention is now focused elsewhere. The mother, quite naturally, will be fussing around the new baby, attending to its every whim and taking a delight in its every action. This kind of extreme emotional response may have been only previously experienced in the first flush of a love affair. Not only has the child, therefore, stolen away the attention, but he has achieved a position with the mother perhaps only previously attained by the father.

In addition to the emotional effects of this, the father also has to watch, and appear to share and enjoy, the physical bond between mother and baby. This is at its height in breast-feeding – a fact that can arouse obvious sexual emotions in the father. The final straw for the father may well be that, in the height of his emotional turmoil, he is not enjoying a sexual relationship with his partner. The one place where he might expect to get the undivided attention of his partner, namely in bed, is now the scene of either exhausted sleep or breast-feeding.

The problem is supposed to be especially acute in younger men, and it's clear to see why. There's not easy answer on overcoming the dangerous emotion of jealousy. The advice offered by others is twofold.

First, recognize it for what it is. You're not failing to love your new child and your wife is not falling out of love with you. It's only natural for the mother to be closely bonded with the new arrival, and your understanding of this fact will help the situation.

Secondly, talk to your partner about it. Undoubtedly she will give you the verbal reassurance you require, although you must remember that she might not be able to respond physically quite in the way you would wish.

One father, although not talking about male jealousy, spoke about his resentment of the presence of his child in the early days. His answer was to look at the baby and remember just how helpless it was, and how much it depended upon the care of both himself and its mother. This, he explained, put what he called his 'understandable but unreasonable selfishness' in perspective.

SHARED DIFFICULTIES AND POSITIVE THOUGHTS

Most of what has been said so far suggests that it is not easy to make a rapid return to the kind of sexual relationship that was enjoyed before a pregnancy and birth. Most of what fathers had to say does support this view. Two other factors are relevant and were mentioned by some fathers. The first is that it only needed time for the situation to return to a satisfactory state. The second is that love-making is always slightly different after the birth because a new overall relationship exists. One father put it quite simply.

66 We were no longer the same. Although we made love as regularly as before, it had a new intensity. We didn't think much about new positions and exotic locations but we actually found a greater satisfaction in what we were doing, more calmly and more lovingly. We had matured. How much was due to the birth of our child I'm not sure, but the coincidence is too great to ignore. **99**

Without underestimating the serious and genuine comments of the father just quoted, there may also be practical reasons why love-making is neither better nor worse, but just different.

66 We had Michael in the same room as us for the first eight or nine months of his life and during that time we were very reluctant to do anything too adventurous in our love-making for fear of waking him up. His presence in the room certainly affected us, especially if either of us heard him cough or cry out. **99**

66 I'm not saying it was a problem – but it was a fact that I had great difficulty in making love knowing there was somebody else in the room. I just didn't like it. **99**

❝ As for sex in the months immediately after Kerry's birth, we were both too knackered to think about it. Whenever we got a few moments' peace and quiet we used to satisfy our greatest desire – we would sleep. **❞**

WHAT SHOULD WE BUY FOR BABY?

Earlier in the book we looked at the likely cost of the whole business and what might be usefully purchased before your baby's arrival. The message was that things may not be as bleak as you think. If you were able to follow some of the advice and bought or were given a lot of things before the baby's birth, such as prams, bottles, cots, clothes and so forth, then the first year of your baby's life may be quite inexpensive. There will doubtless be the essential items that you have forgotten, and a few treats that you decide you would like to buy, but generally the expense can be controlled. There are some continuing costs such as nappies (if you are using disposable ones), milk preparations (if your partner is not breast-feeding) and the ointments, powders and soaps that your baby will need. However, if you so choose you can enjoy a little respite from the spending that may have characterized the period of pregnancy and will, probably, be a feature of the future as your child grows.

One factor that may have caused some concern, namely the loss of an income, may be compensated for by a reduction in your social activities. Also, your partner will be eligible for child allowance, £7.25 per week at the time of writing.

If you have some money available, and assuming you have stocked up on all the basics, there are, naturally, many things in which the manufacturers would like to interest you. What are the experiences of other fathers?

AIDS TO PLAY

Your child will be developing in many ways. During its first year it will certainly learn to play; it may also be walking and talking. There are many opportunities to spend money on aiding development, the effectiveness of the expenditure varying greatly from child to child. In the role of father you may find that you are not involved in the weekly purchase of essentials; your contribution may lie in the provision of the stimulating toys and games than can be so helpful to a young child.

❝ The first lesson we learned was that our child's tastes were very different from our own. Whereas we favoured wooden toys with subtle colours, Cheryl went for anything made out of brightly coloured plastic. It's only natural, I suppose, but a bit disappointing. We've got a bag full of wooden bricks and cars that we hope she will like when she's older. **❞**

❝ The simplest things made her laugh, and of course it didn't matter that it was badly designed, made in Hong Kong and looked simply horrible. **❞**

These two fathers both went on to attest to what has now become something of a child-rearing cliché, that children will play more with the box and wrapping than the toy they contain. This was so patently the case that some parents took to providing their children with toy boxes full of household items such as plastic pegs, yoghurt pots and audio cassette holders. The children thoroughly enjoyed themselves. Of course, one feature of properly manufactured toys is that they will have been made to conform to certain safety standards; this will not be the case with pegs, for example. Commonsense must prevail in providing unusual toys.

Fathers frequently found themselves quite involved in buying toys and other aids to development. This was explained in one case as being a result of the mother doing all the shopping for essentials, so that the father became responsible for the 'luxuries'.

In providing playthings for the child parents sometimes have one eye on the future.

66 We were keen for Cecilia to play an instrument and generally to
enjoy music, but we didn't want to appear pushy or over-
anxious. Our policy was to give her every opportunity to listen
to music, especially while she was enjoying a period of play, and
to let her handle any toy that made a musical sound. This meant
letting her play with rattles and bells and also some more
advanced musical toys. We even had to grin and bear it while she
dribbled on a very expensive guitar and, when she was a bit
older, chewed the end away of a treasured recorder. We wanted
her to see these things as toys and not precious items that are
kept locked away. We were pleased with the results. **99**

The same policy was adopted by another set of parents with regard
to books. Although the child was encouraged to turn pages and
look at brightly coloured pictures, the book was not taken away if
the child chewed it, scribbled on it or inadvertently ripped it.

THE DEVELOPMENT OF STANDING AND WALKING

Toys, whether or not of the recognized variety, help many aspects
of the child's development. Some of the most popular purchases
during the first year were not toys but aids to standing and
walking. If you are having to think carefully about the budget then
it may be worthwhile putting some money aside for a baby walker
or bouncer, or one of the trolleys that enable the child to push and
walk. With any of these items, do check that your house or flat is a
suitable venue for them. Uneven floors, deep carpets and unpro-
tected fires may be dangerous with walking toys, and some houses
are ill equipped to use a bouncer without a special hook being
inserted in the ceiling.

If you can try out any of the items first, or better still can
borrow or hire them, then do take the opportunity. The stage
during which any of the aids to physical development will be
useful will last only a couple of months.

Toy libraries, toy-exchange clubs and second-hand purchases
were all recommended by fathers. It's the parents, not the
children, who insist on certain brand names and particular shops.

A final point, made forcefully by a couple of fathers, is that the first year of a child's life is when to start financial planning for the future. Expenditure can be kept down at this time and there may be some money available for establishing savings accounts, insurance policies or fixed-term investments in the child's name. The first year or so will be the expenditure holiday. As one father put it, aptly summarizing future possibilities: 'It can't be long before infants go on skiing trips.'

---

the first eighteen months – fathers' top ten toys

· those that seemed to help in developmental terms
  · a trolley to push
  · rattles with suction pad bases
  · all kinds of books
  · an 'activity bear' or 'activity centre'
  · shape sorters

· those that provided long hours of fun
  · set of different-sized hoops on a post
  · teddy bears and all manner of cuddly toys
  · toy telephone
  · balls
  · 'pop-up' toys

the next eighteen months – fathers' top ten toys

· those that seemed to help in developmental terms
  · jigsaws
  · books
  · paints and crayons
  · a xylophone
  · a tricycle

· those that provided long hours of fun
  · miniature cars, planes, people etc.
  · a toy tea set
  · sand pits
  · plastic windmills
  · clothes for dressing up

WHAT IF I DON'T LIKE MY CHILD?

Most fathers find no difficulty in experiencing and expressing undying and unwavering love for their children. This emotion is frequently sparked into life by the birth and is later fuelled as the children learn to smile, laugh and, best of all, say 'Dad' for the first time. Sadly, some fathers find difficulty in achieving such a happy state. At best their love or joy is only a fleeting emotion, at worst they have almost no positive feelings at all towards their offspring.

In a few cases there may be deep-seated problems in the father that block the path to a happy relationship with the child; such situations are beyond the scope of this book. In other cases, however, there are understandable difficulties that can be overcome; some fathers were generous enough to share their experience of this situation.

THE OBVIOUS REASONS

As discussed elsewhere, the arrival of a new baby is a major upheaval. Often the upheaval places a strain on the relationship between father and mother; their social life will be disrupted, their sleep interrupted and their finances adversely affected. Bearing this in mind, perhaps it's unsurprising if the originator of the problems comes in for some reproach or resentment.

The new child may also be seen by the father as a threat to his relationship with his partner. It's often claimed that some men marry women who will mother them. How will such a man feel if his partner suddenly becomes mother to someone else as well? Rejection and jealousy are possible emotional offshoots of such emotional immaturity

Another cause of difficulty is the appearance and behaviour of the new baby. Although it may sound surprising to some, there are fathers who are unprepared for a child that is wrinkled, hairless and noisy. They don't like the rather unsocial way in which the child performs all its functions and they can't come to terms with its helplessness. This problem may be exacerbated if the father had nurtured some ideal which remains unfulfilled by the birth. The father may imagine himself as the object of hero-worship and devotion – this may indeed happen later, but the newborn child is incapable of such emotions – or it may simply be that the father has wanted a son and he gets a daughter. For one father this last problem began moments after the birth.

> **"** I can well recall the moment when Polly was placed in my arms in the hopsital. I hoped at the time that it didn't show but I recoiled when I was presented with the rather bloody and very noisy little bundle. I couldn't relate what I was holding to anything I had done. I seemed to feel that she was somebody else's, nothing to do with me. I really wanted to leave the room, go home and have a shower and a sleep. What made it worse was my wife and the midwife both saying how wonderful this baby looked and how lucky I was. I knew I should not be thinking in this way, and that made it worse. **"**

Did this father make his position worse by worrying about what he thought he should be experiencing? This raises the old question of 'paternal feelings'.

UNREALISTIC EXPECTATIONS

Those so-called 'paternal feelings' can be a problem during both the period of pregnancy and the early months of a child's life. As a first-time father you will probably find that people are expecting a lot from you. This may be in the form of extra help for your wife, extra money for the family funds, or a lot less of what you enjoy doing. In the midst of this you are supposed to find room in your heart and mind for love, devotion and unstinting understanding for someone you've known for only a few days or weeks. And not only that, if you don't show these proper emotions you may find friends, relatives and other fathers thinking you are callous, hurtful and unfit for your new role in life. The pressure can build up, and this will only make the situation worse.

> **❝** I spoke to an old friend about kids and he said, quite seriously, that in his opinion they were a waste of time until they were about four or five years old. His comments stuck with me and, while not exactly sharing his views, I know what he means. During the first couple of years with our Gemma I used to cart her around, feed her, kiss her goodnight and do all that stuff. But I never really felt we had much of a relationship. It was a fairly undemanding and not unpleasant duty. What alarmed me were the other fathers I met who took a kind of pride in swearing how strong their attachment to their children was. These fathers would "willingly lie down and die" for their children and would "go to the ends of the earth" for them. I used to worry about how I felt.
>
> Eventually I just fell into a pattern of pretending that my love was stronger than it really was. It was easy to do, as everybody was pleased to hear you say how happy you were and what a great blessing your child was. Ironically, things changed so that it ended up being the truth. I simply grew to love my child as she grew older. I now know that I would be totally devastated if anything should happen to her and I look forward eagerly to the moments we can spend together. But at first it was difficult and I did pretend to love her more than I really did. **❞**

By disguising his true indifference this first-time father deflected a lot of possible criticism and questioning. And happily it allowed him time to develop a relationship that came good after a couple of years. He certainly avoided the pressure felt by one father who, having openly expressed his misgivings about having children, found two sets of friends discussing him as the 'man who disliked his children'. There's a world of difference between having genuine doubts about your suitability for a particular role in life and actively disliking your own children. Unfortunately, some people don't always perceive this.

It's reasonable to compare the bond between father and child with that between husband and wife. It is generally expected that strong and special love should exist. If, for whatever reason, that love does not exist then the pressure starts to mount. If we were able to replace expectation with hope then the situation would be very different. If we only 'hoped' for strong and special love then we might not become so disappointed or alarmed if it did not occur. The experience of so many happy couples is that their love changes and matures. The experience of fathers and children is just the same – only it sometimes seems hard to confess to that fact.

> **“** When our first child was born I was very busy and often used to be away from home for days, or even weeks, at a time. The birth brought a special glow and I loved talking to people about "my little girl". In all honesty, though, I didn't mind being away from her. And when I did get home I felt that she was in the way as I really wanted to spend time with my wife. I found I liked my daughter best when she was asleep – and I felt bad about that.
>
> On one trip home my wife asked how I felt about our daughter. She had obviously noticed something. After some persuading I told the truth, and much to my surprise, my wife confessed to feeling very similar. I had thought that because I didn't see my daughter much I hadn't grown to love her – my wife thought she didn't love our daughter because she saw too much of her!
>
> Fortunately we were able to talk about it together. Our conclusion was that we just expected too much. Our child couldn't give much back at her young age. We would have to be patient.
>
> I don't know exactly how the change took place but I can tell you that, when our daughter recently went away on a school holiday, we were gloomy for a whole week. Having spent months trying to learn to accept her into the family we

were going to have to spend years learning how to let her go **"**
again.

Perhaps this father solved his problem by sharing it with the person who could be most understanding – his partner. But equally important was the acceptance by the parents that they should not expect much back from their daughter – not, at least, at her young age.

When two people form a love bond it is normally the result of both of them needing something from the relationship and both of them putting something in. With very young children the traffic is largely one-way. Perhaps it is no wonder, therefore, that some fathers' early expectations remain unfulfilled.

WHAT CAN BE DONE TO HELP?

Saying that you shouldn't expect too much, and finding fathers who grew to love their children as they wished over a period of time, may provide some comfort. There may still, however, be an emotional void that needs filling as quickly as possible. Some fathers found 'remedies' for their problem that seemed to help create the attachment to their children for which they were looking.

" The best moments for me were those when I would feed Tom. This would normally be one of his last feeds of the day and frequently resulted in him falling asleep in my arms. Penny would take the opportunity of having a few moments to herself so Tom and I would be alone.

I used to look at him and realize just how much he depended on Penny and me. He was forced to be completely trusting. His food, clothing, comfort and everything else came from us. In the most simple terms, without us he could not survive. This realization was the important thing for me and I recommend any father who doesn't understand this relationship with his child to think about this for a few moments. **"**

Without these moments of reflection, this father confessed to great difficulty in forming a bond with his child in its early days. The fact that the child could give so little to his parents was compensated for by its overwhelming needs.

Observing and reflecting was the remedy of another father.

> ❝ In the heat of the action, namely when the baby was crying, when I was changing her nappy, bathing her or when something else was happening to raise the temperature, I would be heartily fed up with the idea of fatherhood. Why couldn't I sit down, pour myself a drink and have a quiet read? But I knew that I had a child, by choice, and that I was going to do the very best I could for it. What I wasn't sure about was how I was going to form a loving relationship with the child and not just treat the whole process as a duty.
>
> The first thing was to try to enjoy the chores, and the second was to find moments when the chores were not the most important thing. The first aim was not easy but the second ambition was achieved by spending time with the baby when she was awake but not needing anything. For a few moments every day (and the amount of time grew with every passing week) Kyle would happily lie on her back and look around her. I would talk to her, tickle her and generally fuss over her. I would imagine that she was responding to my talk and would have long conversations with her, me taking both parts. Today she's five years old and we still try to find a quiet time together during each day, normally to read or just talk. Those early sessions undoubtedly put me on the road to forming a great relationship with her. She became a person and not just a chore. ❞

Whichever way you look at the problem, the passing of time seems to be a great help. In this respect comparisons can, again, be drawn between the bond existing between parent and child and that existing between great friends or sexual partners. One encouraging factor when falling in love as an adult is people telling you that you look good together or 'make a lovely couple'. Comments like these can help a relationship to flourish. For one father this was the 'remedy' for his previously indifferent feelings towards his son.

" It came as a surprise to find out how interested people were in me when I had Jason with me. If we visited shops or public places, or if we popped round to see friends or family, the welcome always seemed particularly warm. I suppose there's still something rare about seeing a man alone with a young baby.

I enjoyed the attention and chose to take him out with me as often as possible. There were no objections raised at home to this policy! I'm sure it was this that helped me start to relate properly to Jason. I used to chat to him in the car, enjoying his company when out walking or driving and jokingly discussed him with others as if he were a mate and not my three-month-old son. The responses from others were great. I would hear comments about how well we got on together and, embarrassingly, once had myself held up as a shining example of how a father should behave. There's no doubt it all helped, although ironically I started taking him out as an excuse to cool off from some of the stresses at home. "

3

LOOKING FURTHER AHEAD

YOUR DEVELOPING CHILD

The development of youngsters is a great problem area – frequently more so for the parents than the children! In particular, parents are beset by comparisons. Comments such as 'Judy can't walk yet but *you* could walk well before your first birthday' are likely to cause both anxiety and irritation. In addition, everybody wants to have their say, and everybody appears to be an expert.

Two basic questions seem to exist in the minds of parents: what is the best way to help, and when should one expect certain developments? To compile a list of 'answers' would both compound the problem described above and would be contrary to all the advice received from the interviews for the book. There is no strict timetable for development and there are no methods by which you can guarantee that your child achieves a certain milestone by a particular age. Take the very different experiences of these two fathers, for example:

> **❝** Kerry was very interested in books, right from an early age. Around the time of her second birthday I can recall sitting night after night, going through story books. She would turn the pages and say what she saw in each of the illustrations. She had a large vocabulary and could relate pictures of things to what they really were. So we could see a picture of a tree in the book and she would say "tree" and then point outside to a real tree in the street. **❞**

“ When she was about two Mary was a proper tearaway. She seemed to have almost no ability to concentrate. We had given her a number of so-called educational toys where bricks fit into certain shapes and can be arranged in sequence, but she showed no interest in them whatsoever. I often tried to get her to sit with us for a few moments, perhaps when she was on her way to bed, but she didn't really want to know. She would rush around like a mad thing, jumping up and down, doing forward rolls I remember, until I took her up to bed. She knew what to do with books but would turn from the front cover to the back in one movement and then jump off my lap looking for something else to do. **”**

Of course, it's no surprise to see that children do things differently, but the reason for including the above is that the two fathers speaking are recalling their children of about twenty-five years ago. Both girls now work with books for a living – and show no difference in their attitude to or aptitude for their work.

With some children reaching Olympic standard in swimming or gymnastics by the time they are thirteen or fourteen, and others (not many) getting their maths degrees by about the same age, it would clearly be hopeless to provide a prescriptive list for stages of achievement. However, the following may be useful as a list of what is likely to come in what order, and how certain things worked for certain parents in assisting the process of development.

Below is a brief summary of some of the more important facets of a child's development. The list is not exhaustive, but covers areas of general interest and concern. Aspects of physical development are tackled first, followed by some examples of the development of social skills. For quick reference the headings are as follows:

The hands
Sitting, crawling and walking
Teeth and hair

Eating and growing
Playing
Talking
Toilet training and other social skills

As will become clear from the selection of fathers' comments provided, there are many additions to these general guidelines. Furthermore, the suggested ages by which milestones of development are reached must be seen as average ages. Finally, before looking at the following notes, it must be remembered that children who are well advanced in one skill or ability are often slow in another area of development – just like adults.

If you have serious doubts about your child's development in any particular area, then consult a doctor. Do not go on the opinions or experiences of other parents. Your GP will be able to give you details of the regular child assessment clinics held in your area.

THE HANDS

Often one of the first things parents notice about their young baby is the way it will grip anything placed in the palm of its hand. Naturally, parents like to offer their fingers for the purpose; holding hands with your one- or two-day-old child is a great sensation. Unfortunately this is just a simple reflex action, not a sign of affection, although controlled hand movements do develop very quickly and provide a number of interesting stages to look out for.

Quite naturally, as the child becomes older so the ability to undertake more difficult manual tasks increases. From the stage described above to the time the child is about three years old there will be a steady procession of achievement. At three years the child will probably be able to manage small buttons, untie knots and play games demanding considerable dexterity such as marbles or tiddly-winks (beware – marbles and tiddly-winks are not the best games for the very young as the bits tend to get eaten!)

The following is a list of interesting stages that you might like to look out for. The order in which they occur may vary a little from child to child. A typical child will manage the first stage by about the age of six months and the last at about two years. But don't worry about how things work out; you will probably know several adults who can barely manage the last stage!

1 Open and close the doors on toy cars or lift the flaps on 'pop-up' books.

2 Place one brick on top of another and manoeuvre shapes so they fit into appropriate holes.

3 Use the hands for social skills like waving and pointing.

4 Use pencils and crayons in a deliberate way.

5 Transfer items from one hand to another while being dressed.

6 Test out hand-holds on heavy items before choosing the most convenient grip.

SITTING, CRAWLING AND WALKING

Perhaps the list should include running, jumping and climbing, because once they get going there's no stopping kids. However, the age at which children do reach these particular milestones may vary a great deal from one child to another – with no detriment whatsoever to the child in later life.

The normal sequence of events is as follows. The first stage can begin only once the child is capable of holding its own head in an upright position.

1 Sitting upright for short periods while supported by cushions or while propped in the corner of a sofa or chair.

2 Sitting unaided and sometimes using the hands for balance.

3 Making attempts to move by shuffling forward on its bottom or by stretching out the hands from a lying position.

4 Crawling, or bottom-shuffling, in one of a variety of styles.

5 Standing while supported by a person or specially designed walker/bouncer.

6 Standing still, unaided.

7 Walking around items, like the edges of a sofa, while holding on.

8 Walking, or rather tottering, around.

Fathers will soon notice where the term 'toddler' comes from when the child moves on from the last stage.

There are numerous points to qualify in the above list. First, it's

Starting to move

· watch out for access to potentially dangerous areas:
  · the road outside
  · stairs
  · glass doors
  · medicine cupboards
  · glass storage jars, bottles etc.

· check that the main hazards are guarded
  · the fires
  · the oven
  · electric sockets
  · steps from one room to another
  · windows

· and don't forget that babies and toddlers can (and do):
  · pull electric cords (bringing down lamps, kettles etc.)
  · sit behind closed doors waiting for adults to open them
  · try fighting with your pets
  · attempt to stand up holding onto unstable furniture items such as stools, bedside tables etc.
  · turn on hot taps and check the water temperature

· above all, use commonsense

important to note that many children don't go through a crawling stage. They find it easier to go from sitting to upright than sitting to lying down. Second, the use of baby walkers (circular frames on wheels) or baby bouncers (elasticated slings hung from the ceiling or door frame) can be a great help in developing a child's abilities on two legs, but don't use them until the child is ready; it will be quite clear when discomfort is being experienced. Third, the ages at which these events occur can vary enormously, with proper walking, perhaps the most exciting stage, beginning at anything from eight to eighteen months.

> **❝** As soon as Chloe could walk we forgot how worried we had been before. From being unable to stand on her own to charging around the flat for hours on end had happened, it seemed, just overnight. Looking back we were probably over-anxious about the whole thing. However, as soon as she could walk we soon found something else to worry about, namely the times she would fall and apparently give herself the most awful knocks on the head. If our experience is anything to go by, children are almost indestructible, although the same cannot be said for the many household items that came into Chloe's reach once she could get around on two legs.
>
> For me, Chloe became a young person, more than just a baby, once she could walk. It seemed to help her develop in a number of other ways. **❞**

The above quote is included to reinforce, yet again, the point that the process of development varies from child to child. Chloe's father felt that her new-found ability to walk encouraged his daughter to progress in other ways too. This is the opposite to the way in which many children develop. It is frequently noticed that being able to walk is such a great thrill for kids that they put all their energies into it and development in other areas slows up. 'Early walker – late talker' is a commonly expressed view.

TEETH AND HAIR

Your child's teeth will probably be a talking point, so it is worth knowing a little about their development. The arrival of teeth often brings about a change in appearance – from looking essentially baby-like to having more adult characteristics. However, the arrival of teeth may also mean some discomfort for the baby, leading possibly to sleepless nights and fractious days.

This ill temper is quite understandable when you remember how you feel with toothache. The teeth are breaking through the gums and causing inflammation. Some relief can be provided by rubbing a soothing gel on the affected gums.

It might appear to new fathers that the whole area of development is a lottery – almost anything can happen at almost any time. Well, it's just the same with teeth. Children may get their baby, or milk teeth even in the womb, although this is uncommon. Conversely, some children do not even get all their first teeth but go on directly to their permanent teeth. It can be reasonably expected that a baby will grow its lower front middle teeth first, at around six months to one year. These will be followed by the equivalent teeth in the upper set. They steadily acquire the rest, normally achieving the first set of twenty teeth by the time they are two and a half or three years.

This book has tried to avoid providing general health advice because there is simply so much of it, and it is already well explained in any number of other books. However, one point in which fathers often seem interested is when to start cleaning teeth. The answer is as soon as possible, with a soft baby toothbrush and mild toothpaste. It helps the development of the gums and encourages good habits for later on.

As for hair, the story is much the same. People love talking about it, especially in the new baby, but there is precious little you can do about it. Whether your child has hair or not at birth bears no relation whatsoever to how its hair will be later in life. Hair comes, and goes, at its own pace. Similarly, the colour and shape of the hair is out of your control; hair frequently changes, so blond babies end up with dark hair, and curly-haired youngsters finish with straight hair as adults.

EATING AND GROWING

Your young child will spend a lot of time having feeds. The pattern of change in feeding depends very much on whether, and for how long, your partner decides to breast-feed. In general you can expect a sequence as shown below. Mixed feeding will begin at around three to four months. The final stage will probably be reached at about eighteen months to two years. How long you continue with bottles and how long your partner breast-feeds are matters of choice; only if your child starts showing signs of hunger do you need to review your policy.

The changeover from baby foods to regular foods will be facilitated if you have a food processor or blender.

1   Breast- or bottle-feeding, with feeds gradually becoming larger and further apart.

2   Weaning begins with the onset of mixed feeding (i.e. milk and baby foods).

3   A move to more regular foods, with fewer baby preparations and milk. This may coincide with your baby being able to hold its own bottle when drinking and being able to eat food without letting it all drop out of its mouth.

4   The changeover to a diet similar to that of the adults in the house. The child will also be able to use simple cutlery and a cup (with a specially designed lip at first).

The order of development is fairly logical. Parents often try to hurry the child along to feeding itself since this saves such a lot of time. There is no harm in this, providing care is taken to give the child sensible foods at all times and you don't mind the mess!

Associated with all this feeding activity will be an increase in the weight of the baby. In the early days after the birth the midwife, and then the health visitor, will check your child's development. After that you need to keep an eye on matters yourselves. It is important to remember that babies who start out small can gain weight quickly, or can remain small; babies who put a lot of weight on in the first few months can lose it again very rapidly or can carry that weight for a long time.

As a rough guide, a baby may gain about seven ounces each week in the first couple of months of its life. It should be fairly obvious from comparisons with other children if your child is either too small or overweight. Check with a doctor if you are in doubt, and don't rely on charts that say what weight your child should be at a certain age.

PLAYING

Play is very important for young children and is an area where fathers often feel they can make a significant contribution. As children play they learn about themselves and the world, so it's important to give your child things to play with that vary in size, texture, construction and so on.

Common sense will tell you which toys are most suitable for your child at any particular age. Your main concern should be to ensure that the toys are washable and safe. Of course, 'toys' need not be expensive items bought from high-street shops. Plastic kitchen utensils, cardboard boxes, piles of computer paper and rags will all interest a young child. It's worth thinking about what 'toys' your child might enjoy in the future, for example books, musical instruments and sports equipment. If you can spare some old or broken items of this nature your child may see these as good fun and to be enjoyed, and not, as is the danger, as precious things reserved only for adults.

A child's play will develop, but not in noticeable steps. Progressing from rattles to plastic bricks and puzzles, and then on to toys which demand more imagination (cars, planes, dolls, shop sets etc.), your child will move gradually at its own pace. Playing with other children may bring significant advances. Toys will become favourites for a while and then be discarded; this was found to be especially true of the type of educational toy consisting of certain shapes which fit only in certain holes. The child might struggle with it for some weeks, but once the technique has been mastered the toy ceases to be of interest.

Lastly, it's worth pointing out the benefits of fathers actually playing and not just providing the means for play.

> ❝ I never seemed to have time to play with Jack at first. But as he got a little older, and I realized what fun it was, I used to aim for about half an hour a day. It is so relaxing, lying there on your stomach making up piles of bricks while your baby knocks them over again. I think I had much more fun than Jack. The best thing is that you have no worries or responsibilities while you're playing. Also, the habit of play has lasted, so Jack and I still spend a lot of time together playing. I think our relationship is stronger because we play together. ❞

It was mentioned above that you should be wary of comparisons. Children do not develop at the same rate. Nowhere is this advice more apposite than in the matter of speech. Some children will be chattering away soon after their first birthdays while others will be three years old or more before they are saying clearly recognizable and correctly pronounced words. Given the right environment, the child will develop speech when it's ready. There's probably more than a grain of truth in the suggestion that the great scientist Einstein said nothing for three and a half years and then came out with a complete and perfectly constructed sentence of twenty words.

Pressure can come from parents who fear that slow development is a reflection of unstimulating home life. Other parents may increase their misgivings by describing how well their own child is talking. Don't let such comparisons worry you. Anxiety will not improve matters.

Since speech develops as a result of listening to others, this should tell you how you can help the process of learning. Try to talk carefully to your child, pronouncing words distinctly and separately. Try also to listen to anything that your child says. But don't rush him.

It is possible to suggest only a very general timetable of development. More important than looking for achievements in speech is making sure that your child hears properly. Speech will never follow easily if hearing problems exist. Your health visitor will undertake basic tests which you can copy at your convenience. However, you should alert your doctor or health visitor if:

1 Your child does not make 'ooh' or 'aah' sounds by three months.

2 Your child does not recognize 'no' or its own name by the time it is eighteen months.

3 Your child is making no attempts at speech by two years.

TOILET TRAINING AND OTHER SOCIAL SKILLS

This last section is just to note a few things that you don't really need to worry about for a while!

Potty training is the big one, and can cause anxiety in parent and child. Most parents will advise forgetting about it until your child is at least fifteen months. It's up to you. But even if you decide to wait until your child is two years old you won't be creating any problems, just costing yourself more in nappies.

Your child will gain other social skills such as table manners, sharing and giving, the ability to make friends, patience when people are talking and a whole lot more, in his or her own time. Of course, you play a vital role in influencing *what* happens, but you will find it very difficult to control *when* these things happen. Both parents should exercise patience and perhaps restrain each other if too much anxiety is shown.

If you are in tune with your child you will know when it is ready to take a step forward; don't worry about the neighbour's child.

ARE UNUSUAL WORKING HOURS A PROBLEM?

Defining 'unusual' in modern society is difficult, since the recent past has witnessed numerous changes in patterns of employment. Today it is common to find fathers working at home, or mothers working away from the home. Equally commonplace are unemployed or self-employed fathers, or those involved in working shifts, long or unsocial hours, or in jobs requiring extended absences from home. Each pattern of work produces special conditions and characteristics. Taking, for the purposes of the discussion, the weekday working father away from home from about 8.30 a.m. to 5.30 p.m. every day as the norm, what types of unusual patterns of work troubled fathers as they planned and experienced family life?

THE STAY-AWAY FATHER

It's not uncommon for fathers to spend about half their lives out of the home because of work commitments. Several of the fathers interviewed for this book undertook daily commuting journeys that entailed leaving home before 7.00 a.m. and not returning until 7.00 p.m.; others, frequently self-employed, were away for even longer hours, and yet another batch spent extended periods abroad on business trips.

As we will read later, not every father would see this sort of absence from home as a problem. However, it is likely to provide both parents and children with some stressful moments and may result in some longer-term effects on relationships and attitudes. How can parents minimize the possible negative effects of long absences?

Perhaps the most commonly discussed problem time is father's daily homecoming. A period in the day that is highly charged with emotion, when every one of the characters involved is hoping to receive some love, support or understanding but none has much energy left to give. In the common situation where the father is out at work and the mother is at home with the young child, a familiar pattern of need is established. Mothers are looking for a helping hand and an adult to talk to, the children want to show off to their father (but actually *need* bathing and putting to bed), and fathers want to relax, maybe with a shower followed by a drink, and then to tell their problems to a sympathetic ear. It all sounds very selfish, but each party feels they have legitimately earned a period of indulgence. Unfortunately, the moment that has been fondly anticipated all day can be spoiled by squabbling and unhappiness.

The problem is, of course, triangular, and as much to do with marital relations as the father–child bond. Some fathers clearly recognized this and their responses to the situation tended to reflect their understanding of it. Recognition of the problem, however, did not mean that some of the solutions were not rather self-centred.

“ When our child was very young there was no problem. I used to get home about 6.30 and the chances were the baby would be asleep. The first thing I would do would be look at Alice and then ask June how she had been during the day. It was summer and we would sit in the garden and talk over a cup of tea. Perhaps I'm romanticizing but I look back on those times as being perfect.

But in no time at all we had a toddler and the situation was very different. By evening June was exhausted from looking after Alice, and just wanted to sit down. I was tired too, and certainly not ready for the barrage of demands from others when all I wanted was to shower and change. And Alice was normally at her worst, fractious and energetic, whacked out but not yet ready to give in to sleep.

So, often the evening would end in a row. June and I would eat supper, not talking to one another but listening to Alice screaming in her room. Her crying produced extra tension.

My first response to the situation was very negative. I tried to cut down on the number of evenings I came home before Alice's bedtime. I organized squash matches for immediately after work and, quite out of character for me, occasionally stopped with a colleague for a drink on the way home on the pretext of discussing some work problem. It was these early evenings in the pub that showed me how silly the situation was becoming. Instead of talking about work, my colleague and I would both talk about how wonderful our children were!

Eventually June and I talked about the problem and came up with a plan. Now, when I get in, I get ten minutes to shower and change – that's *my* time. Then I spent ten minutes with Alice, just playing around and getting her bath ready. While she is in the bath, which happily she enjoys, June and I sit down with a cup of tea. Following that I get Alice ready for bed, sit with her while she has a drink and sometimes look through a book with her. While I deal with Alice, June is getting some supper together. With any luck we can eat this with Alice asleep.

That's the plan – and it works most of the time. The important thing, I feel, is that we all feel we are getting a little of what we want. From my point of view I get a little rest and also a regular time for developing my relationship with Alice. **"**

A 'regular time' was a common aim among those fathers who were out of the home for long periods on a day-to-day basis. One fairly extraordinary family organized their lives so that they got up at 6.00 a.m. and spent an hour together before father went off on his bike to catch the 7.42 train. This was a large family, which normally included one or more foster children, but toddlers were brought into the routine at about twenty months.

The advantages of having a set pattern of activity were mentioned by fathers in all work situations, but those who were away from their children for long periods were strongest in their support of the idea.

“   The important thing to me was that our two children knew that Dad was reliable. They might forget him for long periods during the day but once evening was approaching they knew that Dad was going to appear and give them a bit of love and affection.

We started with our first child when she was about one year old. My wife and I were keen for our children to enjoy books and reading so I would sit with Maryanne and read (well, rip up actually) old magazines. We started the same routine with our second daughter when she was one. The children are now four and a half and three and still enjoy their story-time, although they now try to insist on separate times instead of sitting together.

My wife and I both agree that the person who benefits most from the regular book at bedtime is me! I find it helps me relax and forget the worries of the day. When I get home my mind is racing with work problems, the jobs I ought to be doing and so on; at the end of story-time I'm thinking about Red Riding Hood and how unimportant the cares of the world are when you're father to such beautiful girls as mine. ”

Like so much in fatherhood, the act of giving ends up with its own special rewards. Unfortunately, the concept of a regular time is not available to all fathers, especially those for whom business means long-distance travelling or for whom economic necessity demands working far away from home. For many of these fathers the absence from children – partners were less commonly mentioned – was frequently a major cause of unhappiness. How to establish a good relationship with children became a major talking point.

“ When they were very young our children didn't notice I was gone. It was only my wife who was a bit depressed. But quite quickly they seemed to grow more aware – and they genuinely missed me when I was away. My wife said that they pined for the rest of the day of my departure. She thinks they could recognize the signs, such as the suitcase in the hall or the extra fondness that my wife and I showed to one another. Knowing that I was going seemed to make them restless and naughty.

Of course, I don't have to deal with their behaviour once I'm gone but I try to make special efforts with them when I'm at home. This probably gives them a very strange impression of family life. One week their mother is doing everything for them, then suddenly she's in the background and Dad is taking them down the park, out around the shops and putting them to bed. But what else can I do without changing jobs? I will continue, I'm sure, acting this way and the children, as they grow older, will probably understand exactly what is happening. **"**

" I don't know how to overcome the problem but I know I have one piece of advice. I am away for about half the year on short and long trips abroad. I used to bring home a gift each for our two children – then aged about two and a half and four – from the country I had visited. My homecoming was soon anticipated, not for the arrival of the father in the family but for the presents. The children became very mercenary about my trips. So now they just get me! If I have brought something back it gets saved for a birthday.

Each time I came home from the rig my wife and I would go on a little spending spree, stocking up on things for the house. We tried to avoid spoiling the children with gifts, and anyway soon found that they had nearly all the toys they could possibly want. But what I did do was spoil them with attention, trying to play with them all the time, fussing over them, taking them out and everything. It soon became clear that they didn't want this much attention from me or from anybody. My willingness to be the loving father, in the short times open to me, was becoming a bore for them.

It hurt a little, to sense that rejection, but I soon got over it. I still spend periods away from home but now, when I'm back, I just try to act normally. Our kids are at an age now when they can tell me to get lost if they want to. **"**

The fathers quoted above have generally approached their absences in terms of a problem and have tried to think of ways of minimize the ill effects on family relationships. But today's society does tend to hold in high esteem those whose work involves business trips abroad. And, of course, travel can be interesting and pleasurable – fathers should not be made to feel guilty for enjoying their work. So perhaps it's not surprising to find some fathers adopting a martyred approach as a response to questions about their children. The following view was expressed by several fathers, normally without much obvious regret and generally unaccompanied by suggestions as to how the situation might be put right.

> **“** Oh, I don't think they know who this strange man is who comes in and sleeps with their mother once in a while. **”**

Those fathers who spent long periods away from their children shared many of the problems faced by fathers who worked irregular hours. Shift work and unsocial hours working meant that it was sometimes harder, although on occasion easier, to organize a family life in which the father had set periods with the children. The mother often had to suffer the consequences, especially in stressful situations such as keeping the children quiet while father caught up on sleep, or trying to spend private moments with her partner while the children were awake and active.

While many absent fathers longed to be at home, those fathers who stayed at home frequently wished they were out of the house!

WORKING AT HOME

More men than, say, twenty years ago now work at home. And the trend to home-based working is unlikely to decrease. For the new father there are the obvious problems, and some unexpected ones too. The major difficulty is, undoubtedly, dividing time between work and household. This may have been a problem before the child's arrival, but the situation can only worsen when a new baby places more demands on your time.

> **“** We had made clear guidelines about work and home long before we thought about having a baby. There were certain

times, and for certain reasons only, when I would come out of the office during the day. When Penelope was born, however, there were suddenly dozens more reasons for me to leave my work and take an interest in what was going on in the rest of the house. There were the times when I wanted to be with her, just for the thrill of it, and times when I thought I ought to be with her when she was obviously distressed or my wife was busy and not able to attend to the baby.

My constant to-ing and fro-ing soon became a problem, both for my work and for the family. My customers would get me on the phone while I was holding a crying baby or my wife would get frustrated as I swept into the room to find out what was the cause of the tears and shouting.

I don't think we have solved the problems yet, but we have made stricter guidelines about when and why I should leave the office. It is very hard, though, to sit there and listen to household crises developing and exploding and not do anything about them. **"**

Fathers who worked at home, or mostly from home, made a division between the situation when their children were very young and when they reached the age of one year or thereabouts. With very young children there was rarely a problem, but with older children, especially those who could walk and/or open doors, the difficulties started to mount up. So much depends upon the particular working conditions in the home that it is difficult to generalize. The only helpful pointer seems to be that fathers found that sticking to a formula was the best policy. At least they, their children and their partners knew what to expect in terms of their physical and emotional contribution to the household during the course of the working day.

Finally, it should be remembered that working at home need not be viewed only in terms of a problem. It can, indeed should, be seen as a great opportunity for a father to develop a full and understanding relationship with his child in its early years at home.

Fathers who work at home normally do so from choice. Those fathers who are forced to be at home for whatever reason, and those few who choose to stay at home as 'house-husbands' present different questions and are looked at in the next section.

WHAT ARE THE MAIN CHILD-CARE OPTIONS?

The pattern of your life for the first few weeks and months of your baby's life may be very different from what is going to happen in the longer term. Working women can often stay at home for several months after the birth without detriment to their position at work or their future statutory rights with regard to National Insurance, pensions etc. Many employers allow men to take a week's paternity leave, and many fathers organize holidays to coincide with baby's early days at home.

This 'honeymoon' period, often a very special and exciting time, is regrettably short-lived. Life goes on, and one or both of the parents, through either necessity or choice, have to consider going back to work. The baby is now a major consideration. How it is going to be looked after, whether either parent is going to make a career sacrifice, and how the daily absence of both parents may affect the child are some of the questions that arise.

GOING BACK TO WORK

Despite the 'changes in society' to which this book refers from time to time, there is no escaping the reality of the situation – that in many cases the father will be expected to continue working while the mother will be left with an option. Deciding how the working and earning structure of a household is organized can be complicated. Many factors, economic necessity and the availability of employment being paramount amongst them, have to be considered. Every case will be different, but if you are going to continue work and your partner is unsure about her position, this piece of advice might be helpful.

“ Fran worked her pregnancy leave so she could have several months off after the birth before going back to work. The only proviso was that she had to tell the company whether she intended returning or not. She did want to return.

After several weeks at home, and having established a good relationship with Poppy, she started to have second thoughts. With about four weeks to go before her return to work she was in a terrible state, really upset at the thought of leaving her baby all day.

Having checked with her personnel department we discovered that she would have to repay much of the salary she had been receiving during the pregnancy leave if she decided not to go back to work. It was very difficult for us, financially and emotionally. We could afford, just, for Fran not to work but the extra repayment was too much. In the event she went back to work for a very unhappy nine months, enough to satisfy the company rules, before leaving for good.

We felt so sure beforehand that Fran would want to return to work that we based all our financial planning around that. I would strongly advise other fathers to mention the possibility of a change of heart to their wives and, if possible, make some financial provision for it. **”**

This couple was caught having to repay money they had received in the expectation of the mother returning to work. Furthermore the mother, prior to the birth, was fairly sure what she wanted to do. If possible, keep your options open and make contingency plans for a change of mind. One problem in all this is that the planning often needs to be done several months before the birth for a situation that will occur several months afterwards. It's hard to predict how you will feel, and hard to know how the costs will work out.

> **66** We costed everything to the last penny and discovered, much to our surprise, just how little we were going to benefit by having Julie at work. When balanced against the cost of taking Jamie to a child-minder every day, and the need for two cars so one of us could pick him up in the evenings, plus all the extra costs of actually being at work, it was barely worth it. The reason she went back was because she liked work and didn't want to miss out on the promotion opportunities that were available at the time. **99**

Many parents don't discover the disadvantages of them both returning to work until some important decisions have already been made. The only thing you can do, if you are fortunate enough to have a choice, is to consider the options and to look at others who have been in your situation.

FULL-TIME HELP IN AND OUT OF THE HOME

Assuming that both parents are going back to work, or that neither parent has the time nor inclination to look after the child on a full-time basis, perhaps the best option available is to hire a nanny or au pair. The former, if hired from a reputable agency or if he or she is not trading under false pretences, will be trained to cope with children. The latter, however, will need careful questioning and vetting before being given any responsibilities with children. Having said that, take nothing for granted. The best qualified nanny may turn out to be hopelessly ill-suited to your needs while an untrained au pair, with all the potential for disaster, may transform herself into Mary Poppins on her first sight of your children.

Ideally you will able to take somebody on following a recommendation from a trusted friend. Failing that, the best thing to do is take the plunge and be prepared to be flexible.

> **66** Our experience was satisfactory. Louise (the nanny) was very good with Charles and I have no complaints on that front.

There were matters, however, over which we seemed to lose control. The times we spent with Charles were too short for us to start "correcting" what Louise had done.

For example, I don't think she managed meal times very well, allowing Charles to get away with bad behaviour and picky eating. Having said that, I wouldn't claim to know exactly when you should start teaching manners, so perhaps I am being a little over-critical. The general difficulty was that of knowing where to draw the line. What should we insist upon and where should we allow Louise the responsibility to do what she thought was best? There were times when we had to lay the law down and she probably thought we were being rather fuddy-duddy, but considering her job was so crucial and that she lived with us for almost three years, everything went very well indeed.

Ideally one wants to set out the requirements of the job at the time of the first appointment; say exactly what is essential and what is desirable. Unfortunately, at that time, you have no idea of what problems areas might arise. Your new nanny probably has much more experience of children than you. **"**

Nannies are, of course, expensive. At the time of writing an average charge for a nanny is £85 per week, so budget for at least £100 out of pocket. This would be either for living in or coming in on a daily basis; additionally, and depending upon the agreement, you will need to provide meals and accommodation. It is almost impossible to be specific about cost; the only sensible advice is to check amongst your friends or pick up the Yellow Pages and ask. So much will depend on the particular nanny that it's hard to generalize about the advantages and disadvantages of such an arrangement. It was often quite minor drawbacks that fathers noticed about having a nanny. In particular, there was the need that some parents felt to ensure that things were in order for the nanny. This meant extra housework, many more clean clothes for the baby than might otherwise have been the case, and only special baby foods where portions of the meals left from the previous day might have been satisfactory.

A much more common way of coping with full-time child care is to send the baby to a nursery or child-minder. Much the same comments apply to these options as to nannies. It's best to ask for recommendations and to think carefully about the cost. Local registration of recognized child-minding services will exist, and going to an accredited person or centre will guarantee certain minimum standards. Many excellent child-minders, however, do work informally and are unregistered; it's your choice. When making a decision it is sensible to visit the location for an inspection at the time of day you will actually be taking your child along.

> **&&** I made a dreadful mistake. Having looked at two possible day nurseries for the child I persuaded my wife to accept the one that was nearer my route to work; I could reach it with only a slight detour. This meant we could still manage with one car. Unfortunately I forgot to think about the traffic in the mornings. The upshot of this was that we had to get up at about 6.30 each morning to give us enough time to get both of us, and more importantly the baby, ready. **""**

The amount of extra effort needed to get a child ready every morning should not be underestimated. The one recurring result of being actively involved in the transport of child to nursery was tiredness. Extra work in the morning and evening, at times when you least feel like it, put a great strain on parents and child alike.

Another problem that faced parents using a nursery was the lack of control over the daily activities of their child. Normally it was possible to insist on such things as a vegetarian diet or wearing an extra vest at all times. Less control was possible in matters of nursery policy, such as attitudes to the sexes or, more practically, when a child sleeps. One father discovered that his one-year-old son slept for about three hours in the afternoon at the nursery, making it impossible for him and his wife to get the boy off to bed in the evenings.

All of what has been said about day nurseries can apply to a crèche, the advantage here being that the parent using the facility will probably be more conveniently placed for dropping off and picking up. Sadly for mothers and fathers, very few companies offer a crèche facility.

A last point worth remembering when envisaging both parents at work is what contingency plans exist for the sick child. It's hard to plan for the unexpected, but you will be lucky if there are not a few days when your young child is too ill to go to a child-minder or nursery. On such days, or in situations where the child is taken ill while away from home, a parent will probably be needed. One point that fathers were quick to mention is that priorities change after the birth of a child. What might seem like an unmissable deadline or the most important business meeting of the year can pale into insignificance when your six-month-old treasure has just cut her hand or caught mumps. Happily, attitudes to fathers are changing slightly, and it's possible that your plight will be viewed with sympathy if you are the only parent available.

USING THE PARENTS' TIME

Whatever method of child care is adopted, a problem arises with the evenings, weekends and other times when the nursery or nanny is not available. The father's position is not the same as if he had been out working all day with the mother at home, because the times in question will be the only ones when both parents can be with the child.

The pressure on the parents to use this time well can be immense. Leaving aside those fortunate enough to afford extra help in the home, the parents will probably want to fit household duties, social engagements, personal activities and looking after their children all into a very short space of time. Compromises and sacrifices are almost inevitable. Fathers found that hobbies such as sports or DIY quickly went by the board. Other jobs that had previously been theirs, such as car maintenance or gardening, were either neglected or given over to professionals.

There were also short-term problems with the children.

66 We found that Saul needed a day to get over the effects of the nursery. Although we were generally pleased with the place, we knew that they let things pass that we would not. For example, at the nursery he would walk around in his socks and nobody would insist on him wearing shoes or slippers. Also, nobody bothered much if he didn't eat his

food properly. Most Saturdays would be difficult as he faced our standards and reacted against them. But by Sunday he seemed to be quite happy at home and, momentarily at least, reluctant to go back to the nursery on Monday.

He went to the nursery on a daily basis for almost four years and is now at school. I don't think it has affected him badly, and he has settled into school very quickly. I think we have been the ones to suffer and now, as we look forward to our second child, we are looking at the possibility of my wife giving up work altogether. **"**

All the above factors are worth considering when viewing the options open to you after the birth of your child. One option, not commonly considered but gaining slightly in popularity, is for the father to stay at home and look after the house and baby – to be a 'house-husband'.

A random survey of those acting as house-husbands suggested that the main reason for choosing this option is economic necessity. Many house-husbands are otherwise unemployed or have partners with far superior earning capacity. Very few seem to choose this role as an alternative to paid work, and of those house-husbands interviewed all explained that they tried to do a bit of paid work (decorating, guitar tuition and writing were mentioned) when they could leave baby with a relative or baby-sitter, or when baby was asleep.

The only problem area for house-husbands, apart from the financial anxieties that some of them faced, was that child-rearing is not generally considered as men's work. Both organized and informal groups that offered help and support were dominated by women; young mothers, mother and baby and NCT post-natal groups, quite understandably, were unsure how to treat a man in their midst. Similarly, baby-changing and other support facilities in clinics, shops and hotels were inevitably provided in the women's toilets or changing rooms. The intention of this book is not to be a springboard for a campaign to change matters, but it is important to point out why some house-husbands have experienced a sense of isolation in their job. And while the novelty value of the situation can be used to advantage, being a house-husband generally means dealing with unforeseen obstacles and occasional outright prejudice.

LOOKING FURTHER AHEAD

The options discussed above will vary in the educational and emotional support they provide. Some child-minders will stick closely to their job description and simply mind your child. Others, especially good nannies, will be a complete mother substitute. You need to decide what is important for your child. As he or she gets older, the options do broaden a little and you may care to plan at an early date for moving your child on to a nursery school or play group (sometimes called play school). These are essentially educationally-based institutions where you can expect your child to receive help in structured play, interacting with other children, artistic expression and physical development. They may be privately run or organized under the aegis of the local education authority. Other parents in the locality will be the best source of information and advice.

The reason for providing information about the various options is to aid your discussions but not to suggest that you should plan your child's daily pre-school life at such an early stage. This father was typical:

> **❝** I asked around among friends and worked out a plan for how we would deal with us both working. It seemed suitable for the child and Yvette, my wife, was happy to fit in with it. What we didn't, and couldn't, plan for was the way our feelings were to change. We had always wanted a child, but in our own time, when we were ready. When Nicky came along we were delighted but still sure that we wanted to continue our careers. Within a month of the birth, however, neither of us could bear to leave her in the mornings. It began to blight our lives, missing her so much every day. Yvette soon left her job completely and I managed to change my duties so I could work from home once a week. **❞**

Wherever possible, maintain some flexibility. The arrival of your child will change your life in so many ways. Although financial necessity or personal ambition may drive you and your partner on, it's just possible that your attitudes and priorities will change.

WHAT ABOUT THE CHILD?

Most important of all, but least able to stick up for itself, your child will obviously be influenced by what happens during its early life. How will a child react to being away from its natural parents for much of its young life? For those fathers in situations where both parents worked the answer was unequivocal – whether using a nanny or nursery, au pair or child-minder, fathers saw no ill effects on their children whatsoever. You may be tempted to comment that fathers would say that, wouldn't they, but to take that view does imply that quite a number of fathers were either badly mistaken or perhaps lying to cover up a sense of guilt.

This book asked only the fathers and not the children, but the fathers interviewed generally appeared to have well-balanced and happy offspring. This book also tackles the situation from the male standpoint; mothers may have a very different story to tell. So there is certainly more to the question than can be explained here. However, the view of fathers is clear. Children do not appear to suffer if both parents work. Some of the positive points about such an arrangement are as follows.

> **❝** We employed a nanny for six days a week so we really didn't spend a lot of time with either of the babies when they were young. But we did take our roles seriously. I set aside periods when I would play with them, take them out or, sometimes, feed and change them. During these times I was always fresh, my attitude was good and the children responded well. How I would have been had I spent all week with them I shudder to think. They got the best of me; I think this applied to my wife too. **❞**

> **❝** I'm sure that the good relationship I have with my children is because I didn't see too much of them when they were growing up. From the age of two or three months they went to a nursery. This was where they did all the mundane things and where they also got disciplined. I mostly played with them, spoke kindly to them and enjoyed their company when

they were relaxed. As a result I became associated with good things and a good time. I'm sure that this early impression they had has been good for our longer-term relationship. **99**

66 There were no young children in the family and very few in the village. Peter greatly benefited from having other kids around him. Also, I'm sure, he learned to mix much better with other people of all ages. Living as we did, some miles from the nearest village, there was a danger of him growing up as a rather solitary young child. **99**

66 We lived on a large estate, in a flat. We didn't have much money, particularly when Jake was very young. The nursery where Jake went was next to what they call a "city farm" so he had plenty of opportunity to see a few trees, plants and animals as he grew up. **99**

66 Of course the child is important, but so are the parents. I never intended, nor could afford, to give up work. If Josephine had stayed at home I'm sure the marriage would not have lasted. She would have been so frustrated and angry about being at home with a young baby. She went back after four months the first time and three months with the second. **99**

CAN I PREVENT MY CHILD BECOMING A BRAT?

The title is not a very elegant one, but it exactly sums up one of the most frequent worries expressed by fathers. If a child is healthy and generally happy, the next most important thing to a father is that he or she is well behaved.

Behaviour becomes more of a problem as the child grows. When it's very young you may describe your child as 'in a bad mood' or 'badly behaved' but you will know that the crying you hear is merely a response to some need or discomfort; the child starts to 'behave' only when it can wilfully call attention to itself by crying, shouting, throwing tantrums or otherwise making its presence felt. Unfortunately, many fathers worry because they feel that they should be able to take steps to prevent shows of bad behaviour. They are also concerned that the approach they have adopted in the past has somehow led to this current state of affairs.

What, if anything, can be done at an early age in an attempt to ensure good behaviour as the child grows?

SHARING THE RESPONSIBILITY

Nowhere was the concept of shared parenthood thought to be more important than in matters of behaviour. This father is talking about his two-year-old, but it's clear that the situation he describes has its roots in the child's earlier life.

   ❝ Trevor used to do all the things that we expected him to. He pulled records out of their sleeves, scribbled on the wallpaper, tore up the papers before I had read them and played with our best china ornaments. None of these things were really bad; we just told him "no" and watched out for a while. More upsetting though were the times when he would refuse to go to bed, smack other children, scream when we tried to put new clothes on him, and pull the cat's tail. With these things, where he knew he was doing wrong, he would get severely told off; if he really persisted, which he often did, we just stuck him in his room.

   His first reaction after a scene would be to run to the other parent for comfort. When he could first talk he would run to mother sobbing "Dad" while pointing an accusing finger at me, or would run to me while shouting "Mum". At first we interpreted this as telling tales and scolded him even more. Of course it was nothing of the sort, just looking for a bit of forgiveness and the chance of a cuddle.

   Although we try to be consistent we find it very helpful that we can play one off against another – if we choose to. It means that one of us can calm him down, and can go back to the scene of the "crime" and explain why he was told off in the first place. **❞**

This type of situation, very common with children, can work only if the child has grown up seeing the parents as equals, with equal or similar responsibilities. The more traditional pattern, in which the mother does the daily reprimanding and the father is responsible for the final judgements and punishments, found little favour with today's fathers. Of course, where the father is away all day there can be the temptation to use him as a threat, but it seems that this is now rarely the case.

As pointed out above, a shared responsibility means that either parent can placate a child. Naturally it would not be sensible to let a child run from one parent to another, knowing that everything that caused one parent to be angry would be forgiven by the other. A united stance will be needed most of the time. But there are occasions when the ability of one or other parent to step into the breach and calm a potentially upsetting situation can be very helpful.

> ** ❝** Before I was a father I used to look at the babies screaming in
> supermarkets or the tantrums of youngsters in the street and
> think "not me!" Although I wanted children I thought that my
> kids would know how to behave, especially when away from
> the home.
>
>   Now, of course, I know better. I think our two children have
> been brought up strictly but there are times when they will not
> listen, and you do not have time for an explanation. That's when
> we give in. For example, we might be out visiting when one of
> them creates bit of a scene because she's not allowed to touch
> something. Nothing I can say can stop the noise but my wife
> will be able to distract the child's attention with something else.
> In that way peace is maintained, neither my daughter nor I has
> had to concede, and my wife scores a point with the children.
> Next time the roles may be reversed. **❞**

Apart from any other consideration the idea of sharing the role of
disciplinarian halves an unpleasant task. Most fathers found that
telling off their children was one of the most upsetting things they
did. They admitted to forgiving them within moments of scolding
them. What was disquieting was that the children seemed to forget
their telling-off literally moments after it happened. Just as children
get well very quickly after an illness, so they recover from the most
severe reprimands with little bother at all.

THE CODE OF CONDUCT

In trying to set limits on what a child can and can't do you are
beginning their preparation for life beyond the home. This was
uppermost in many fathers' minds when they set up their household
'rules'. For, while many fathers could cope with children being
noisy, disruptive and disobedient at home, it was the thought of how
they would behave when away from home that led the fathers to
impose some form of discipline. Of course, with children as young as
those we are considering in this book you can only go so far. Despite

this, there were some points on which fathers showed no compromise, no matter how young the child. This father cites some examples.

> **❝** There were two areas where we began Helen's education from, almost, the day she was born. The first related to safety. With electric plugs and open fires anything and everything connected with them can be dangerous. She could never have mistaken our tone of voice when we found her anywhere near either. The second was to do with food. As Christians we always say grace before a meal and always expect to eat everything that we are fortunate enough to have. We tried to encourage her to eat everything and, as she got older, told her in no uncertain terms that playing with food was absolutely out. **❞**

As the child grows older, he or she will be able to understand a greater range of behaviour parameters. Some parents, in trying to be both consistent and strict, can create a rather unhappy atmosphere. What they are doing is intended to be for the good of the child, but matters can get out of hand. Should you feel this is becoming a problem, this father has some good advice.

> **❝** Life was becoming a bit miserable as every day was a battlefield between June and me and Alex. He was only one year old at the time and I worried that matters would get worse as he grew older. We definitely eased up a bit. I compared it with the time I moved from a size 34 waist trouser to a size 36: I was sudddenly no longer overweight! By letting Alex get away with a few things here and there, suddenly he was not so badly behaved. **❞**

WHAT SORT OF DISCIPLINE?

Taking an interest in behavioural matters presupposes that you might want to do something if your child steps out of line. Codes of conduct are unnecessary items if they have no use apart from measuring how far outside them a child can go. Your regime of reprimands and punishments must be entirely a matter of personal choice, but with the very young child there is only so much that can be done.

The universally accepted method of introducing your child to the concept of right and wrong, good and bad, is the use of the magic word 'no'. More than one father announced, with some guilt, that the first word his child could say was 'no'. This is not so surprising, but upsetting it you were hoping he or she might come out with 'Dad'.

Of course, the word is actually less important than the tone in which it is delivered. Use of a key word to tell your children that they must not do certain things (for whatever reason) is a form of disciplining that can begin very early. Fathers who started out with a fairly strict policy of 'no' meaning just that, and physically removing the child if he or she disobeyed, were happy with the longer-term effects. Two- or three-year-old children responded well to being told 'no', an especially useful weapon if needed when out visiting.

Beyond verbal reprimands you have to consider what else a child might understand during its first year or so. Reasoning with young children seemed to bear little fruit, and the withdrawal of privileges will not normally be comprehensible. One of the remaining options is the use of physical punishment. In the very young child there can surely be no justification for even slight slaps or smacks. They serve only to release the anger felt by the parent. If some form of release, is needed then this father had a couple of answers.

“ We got very frustrated at times. If things got too bad we would stick Alana in her room and close the door. She could scream all she wanted but would have to wait until we were ready before we collected her again. This was when she was about one, and I think it worked well. As she grew older, however, we realized that her room was becoming associated with punishment and she got upset if we suggested she went to it to play or when it was time for bed. There didn't seem anywhere that could be used in the same way; we didn't want to create a punishment cell!

Now, if she has a tantrum because she's not doing what she wants, we join in. We roll around, shout and cry, and smack our hands on our heads. It's great. **”**

While psychologists might not think this very sensible, it does have the advantage of allowing the parents to let off steam too. In so doing it may avoid the build-up of tension that might have a worse effect on the child.

ANXIETY ABOUT BEHAVIOUR

In a book such as this it is possible to provide only a few general pointers. Large tomes have been written dedicated solely to problems of behaviour. Furthermore, by the time your child is approaching the age where bad behaviour really does become a serious matter, you will know him or her so much better and will be more able to formulate your own plans for tackling the problem.

In the early years there is not a lot that can be done. And even if you seemingly 'go by the book' this will not be a guarantee of success. The 'terrible twos' and the 'throttlesome threes' come to nearly all children, no matter how they were treated in infancy.

Naturally you will be worried by bad behaviour, especially if you see the child's social conduct as a reflection of what goes on at home. Your anxiety may well be increased if you are told, as no doubt you will be, that some other child is so well behaved, so polite and never any trouble. Your child, at the time you hear this, will be behaving like a perfect monster. But the only advice can be that all children, like adults, experience ups and downs. Being disobedient is a way of asserting their independence, a very healthy sign if the whole process can be achieved with the minimum of drama and the maximum of good humour. Let this father put things in context:

“ If you think you have problems when your child is very young, just wait until it reaches the twos and threes. And if you think that's bad – when it starts school you're in for a real shock. But was I naughty as a boy? Of course I was. And am I perfect as an adult? Of course I'm not! **”**

THINKING ABOUT ANOTHER?

Many couples plan from the outset to have more than one child. More common, though, are those couples who are keen to have one child and then are happy to wait a while before thinking about another. If you are still awaiting the birth of your first child then trying to decide about more children will be the last thing on your mind; if you've just had your first then you probably won't have time to read this anyway. But if you have plans, however vague, it is worth considering the matter at some early stage, not least because conception can take a long while to achieve, particularly, as we shall see later, in new mothers.

Apart from your own hopes for a family you may be faced with pressures from outside, too.

❝ One thing that happens to most single men with girlfriends is that they get pestered by their married friends about when they are going to get married. Most of the time it is light-hearted banter; some of the time it borders on either serious advice or serious interference. However, the pressure put on single men to get married is much less than the pressure put on married couples to have children.

For staying single you may be called silly, but for intentionally staying childless you are thought of as both selfish and rather stupid. I thought the comments might stop when Kathy and I produced Ben, but no, shortly after Ben was about six months the questions started again. When were we planning to have another, did we now want a girl and how long did we think we ought to leave it before the next one?

In a strange way this kind of social pressure was the most unwelcome I can remember. You don't know what life is like before marriage or before children until you try it. But having another child is different – you have experienced it and are in a good position to make the right personal decision. It really surprised me how insistent friends and family were with their questions. I suppose the enquiries were well-meaning, but we both got very fed up.

I would say it is very important to shut your mind to what people expect and want. There is only one decision in life as important as having a child and that is having another child. Just because you have had one doesn't mean it's now easier or less momentous. The responsibility is just as great and the care and planning should be just as careful as for the first. **"**

That the second child deserves equal care and attention was a point raised by many fathers. Many confessed to not being as excited or interested second time round although, happily, most said that once the child arrived it was just the same as for the first.

But before this situation occurs, most couples face the questions 'why' and 'when'.

DECIDING FACTORS

If either partner remains unconvinced about having a second, the discussions will begin again. This time round, however, the ground has shifted a little; some of the points that were so important the first time are no longer valid.

" The arrival of our first child wiped away all the question marks that existed before his birth. Adam was now with us, so what did it matter that we had argued about whether or not we should have started a family. You can't go up to your child and say we didn't really want you at the time. Thinking about a second, however, was different. Many of the points we had raised first time round were no longer relevant. Caroline, my wife, had "experienced" childbirth. We had made a family. We would have the chance of grandchildren and family life when we got older. So why have another?

The matters we discussed were nearly all related to Adam. No longer were we the important factor in decision-making. Two-year-old Adam had the "casting vote". Whether he would like a sister/brother, whether he would be lonely or spoilt as an only child, and would we devote enough time to him if we had more children, were the main questions in our minds. **"**

The first child obviously plays an important, though unknowing, part in the decision-making. In addition there will be other factors that were important first time round such as the cost, the parents' own ambitions and plans, and the general ability of the household to absorb another member.

Whether or not you try for another is, quite clearly, a personal decision that will be based on emotional as much as practical considerations. Of the fathers interviewed there was not one who would go back on his decision to have, or not have, another child. Most fathers, however, knew that another child was inevitable; the question was simply 'when'. The debate that took place between them and their partners related only to the timing of the next arrival – the decision to try for another had been taken long ago, often before the birth of the first and frequently without any form of structured discussion.

For most fathers the fundamental question was whether to 'get it over and done with' or to wait until the first child was at school or at least away from the home for most of the time. This father was a supporter of the former school of thought.

" You must think about the disruption to your life. You've got no time to yourself, your plans always take second place to those of your children, you're spending more money, your favourite possessions are all hidden in boxes and you spend much of your social life with other parents looking at pictures of kids. If you've got to live like that you might as well minimize the damage and get it over with in a few years. Waiting until Charlie was five would have meant ten years or more with a young child at home. At least with the two-year gap we get some respite after six or seven years. **"**

Child care doesn't stop when your child trots through the school gates for the first time, but the calculation of 'years at home' has some importance. Full-time education does release the parents from some obligations. Don't forget, though, that your child may be able to attend a nursery school, which would shorten the 'at-home' period, or, conversely, that more than one child will lengthen the time.

More positively, having a short period of time between children can mean companionship between your offspring, shared learning opportunities and a chance for the development of close family ties. There are also some more practical considerations.

" Although I didn't total up the costs I'm sure we saved by having two children close together. All the basic equipment was in place. We didn't need a new set of baby clothes, although we bought some, and we had the extras like a baby bouncer, a changing mat and so on. My wife decided to stay off work for a longer, continuous period; she hopes to resume her career when the second child starts in full-time education.

We had two boys and so expect to keep them in the same room for many years to come. Had we had a girl second time round we were planning to use the same room for a quite a while. I don't think it bothers young children. **"**

Sharing a bedroom does become more of a problem with an increased age gap, as might sharing meal times, friends and tastes in television programmes!

Waiting for a while before increasing the family size may sometimes be the result of indecision and sometimes the result of other concerns. Most commonly, though, there are strong reasons why parents choose to delay. Foremost among them is the sheer amount of work connected with the first baby. If you are yet to have your first child you may find this hard to believe, but most fathers, and very likely most mothers, felt they wanted some period of rest before facing the prospect of more sleepless nights, more uncontrollable crying and more of the other less popular happenings of the first few months of a baby's life.

If your partner takes the lion's share of work with regard to your first baby, you must be careful when planning for the second. For, while looking after one young child is hard enough, doing it whilst pregnant, and perhaps unwell, is likely to bring serious problems.

> **"** There were four or five days when Yvonne couldn't cope on her own. I had to take time off work to look after Robert; she was just too ill to get out of bed. Throughout the pregnancy she was tired and suffered many of the classic symptoms such as aching joints, heartburn and nausea. This was such a contrast with first time around when she seemed to "bloom" as we had been led to expect. We didn't seem to have a minute. When we did get some time off we argued. It was a very difficult time. Although there were good reasons for us hurrying along with the second, I sometimes wonder whether the strain on our relationship and Yvonne's health were worth it. **"**

Doctors will tell you that a second pregnancy close to the first can lead to extra stress and tiredness. Those mothers who wait normally enjoy an easier second pregnancy. There can be benefits for both the children, too, if the parents decide to wait.

> **"** In trying to do things right for the first child I realized that I would not have time to do the same if we had two children close together. I believed that the first couple of years of Mark's life were very important for his development. I was not at home for a great deal of the time, but when I was I tried to give him plenty of attention. I would play with him, dress him, bath him, read books to him and would always be the one who went into him at night if he woke up. I knew that I could not give the same level of attention to two children if we had them close together.

> I think that it gets easier as the children get older. They can do more for themselves and need less of your undivided time. **"**

It's easy to see the logic of this view, although others would argue that the second child learns from the first, especially if they are close in age. Another line of thought suggests that the second child can become lazy if the first does a lot for him or her; this is particularly true of speech, where second children are often 'interpreted' by their older sister or brother.

It's clear that nearly every supporting factor for an early second child can be matched by a contrary view supporting a delay in family building. One point of view that many fathers expressed was that the second child's arrival may have marked effects on your relationship with your first. In the typical situation where the mother is the more busily involved with the baby, you will find yourself doing much more with the older child, whether it be getting ready to go out, eating meals, getting dressed in the morning or whatever. A situation of apparent favourites can emerge in which father is identified with the older child and mother with the younger. Emotional ties that are established at this time may never be weakened.

Finally, it's worth pointing out that *planning* for a second is far removed from *having* a second. Conception may take much longer where the partners are tired and where love-making is less frequent than before. Moreover, the woman's body may take a while to get back to normal.

Knowing that there are clear pros and cons for both hurrying and waiting should relieve you and your partner of any pressure. If you have been lucky once then already you are more fortunate than many men, so just look after yourself, your partner and your first child(ren) and hope for the best.

HEALTH CHECK

This is a quick guide to health matters, organized variously by symptom, affected part of the body and illness – whatever seems most useful to the worried father. The listing is not exhaustive, but deals with those matters that arose most commonly in discussion with fathers. For speedy reference, the main headings are as follows.

Crying
Convulsions
Lumps and bumps
Spots
Temperature
Tummy ache
Vomiting

Ears
Eyes
Teething

Cot deaths
Cradle cap
Croup
Encephalitis
Immunization
Meningitis
Whooping cough

*

The section is intended for use when you are anxious about your child. It is hoped that the information will either put your mind at rest or give you some indication of what actions you should take. Like the rest of the 'advice' in this book, the information is based on the actual experiences of parents, although, for obvious reasons, it has been supplemented by details from medical sources. If there is any doubt in your mind about the health of your child do not rely on this or any other book; get proper attention from your doctor.

Two other points for you and your partner to remember are that things always seem worse in the middle of the night, and that children can get better just as quickly as they become ill in the first place!

CRYING is something some babies are very good at, while others don't get much practice. Basically it's a change in the crying pattern which causes concern. If there is not any obvious cause of distress, if baby is clean, not hungry, not too full, and neither windy nor tired, it may be worth taking his temperature and making decisions accordingly. If the temperature is normal but crying persists and he won't settle for you, try another adult if possible; your anxious 'vibes' may be getting through! If there's still no joy, get help. There may be something wrong.

CONVULSIONS may follow high temperature, which is why bringing down a high temperature is important. The muscles react to the nerves reacting to the brain reacting to the temperature of the child – the muscles go into spasm, then relax, jerking and twitching. The whole body, or only part of it, may be affected.

The convulsion itself will not damage the child but he may choke if on his back, so turn him gently on his side and make sure he can breathe freely. Stay with him until the fit passes, call the doctor and try to reduce the temperature by sponging him down with tepid water.

LUMPS AND BUMPS occur on every child, even in the best-regulated families. Sometimes they are the result of illness, but more commonly the product of falling over, being accidentally knocked or tripped or any of the numerous little pitfalls that beset a human less than two feet tall. Obviously you must take reasonable precautions, but health visitors and doctors understand the situation and don't jump to horrific conclusions if children appear with bruises from time to time.

GLANDS tend to provide interesting lumps too. The glands in the neck can go very lumpy if the child has a virus; you must get medical advice, especially if there is a high temperature as well.

MUMPS, of course, is a major lump. Sometimes the glands on both sides of the ear–jaw line swell up together, sometimes only on one side, to be followed, perhaps, by the other when you think that it may be all over. Mumps is an uncomfortable rather than a dangerous condition for a child. It may be slightly painful, and swallowing may be difficult. Very occasionally, complications set in about a week after the onset of the illness. If a fever arises, notify the doctor as there is an outside risk of meningitis. Infectiousness lasts from three days before the swelling until seven days after it has gone down.

SPOTS come in all sorts and shapes and sizes. Some of them indicate an infectious disease; some are mysterious 'non-specific' spotty viruses; some reflect an allergy. In general, when reacting to spots you should bear in mind the following.

● Is anyone else spotty at the moment? Something may be going round.

● Does the child have a high temperature?

● Where are the spots exactly?

● Have you just changed your washing powder/introduced a new food etc.?

The most common types of spotty illnesses are listed below.

CHICKEN POX will entail itchy spots which turn into nasty little blisters, mainly on the face and trunk. Calamine lotion may help to reduce itching; children should be discouraged or prevented from scratching as far as possible. Infectiousness lasts from five days before the first spot appears until all the blisters have scabs.

GERMAN MEASLES (RUBELLA) is nasty (and dangerous)

for pregnant women, but not particularly unpleasant for children. There may be a raised temperature; the flattish, pinky spots appear very rapidly until they resemble a flush, and disappear just as fast. The child will be infectious from seven days before the spots until four days after they have all appeared.

ROSEOLA INFANTUM gives a reddish, flat rash all over the trunk; this appears after several days of fever and is accompanied by swollen glands in the neck. The child is infectious for five days after the spots appear.

MEASLES can be particularly nasty, so treat it cautiously. Even vaccinated children can still get it. It starts with a high temperature and cold symptoms such as a cough, runny nose and watery eyes. 'Koplik's spots' – little white dots inside the cheeks – appear three or four days later. They are followed by dull red spots behind the ears and on the face, spreading to the arms and trunk. Infectiousness lasts from the beginning of the fever until four days after all the rash has appeared.

Some doctors prescribe antibiotics routinely to measles patients to guard against possible secondary infections, which present the major problems with measles. Be watchful – but not too imaginative. Possible secondary infections are unpleasant: conjunctivitis, ear and throat infections, pneumonia, bronchitis and inflammation of the brain.

SCARLET FEVER is an odd one, because it's really a throat infection which just happens to produce spots – little red dots pretty well everywhere except for an area round the mouth which looks very pale as the rest of the skin is flushed. Again it's the risk of secondary infection – ears, kidneys or rheumatic fever – which is the main problem, so see the doctor.

Other spotty complaints include:

IMPETIGO, which is a bacterial skin infection, usually on the face. The spots are like blisters which dry to a hard crust. As it is highly infectious, the patient should have her own towel, etc.

ECZEMA, an often hereditary allergy problem. It looks blistery or scaly, appears on the face or inside the elbows or the knees, and may be aggravated by certain foods or skin preparations. There is a lot of help available for this condition.

NAPPY RASH, a sometimes painful condition when it

becomes severe, causing the baby to cry when urine or faeces meet the tender area. It generally responds to more frequent changes of nappy and the liberal application of cream. Where possible, leaving the baby without a nappy is very beneficial. The health visitor will advise.

SCABIES, a parasitic infestation, which requires medical diagnosis and treatment. It can be dealt with by creams and lotions, but bedding will need to be disinfected.

SEBORRHIC DERMATITIS, which may arise in young babies especially if they have had cradle cap or nappy rash. It appears behind the ears, on the face and at the warm, rubby places such as behind the elbows and the knees, and is aggravated by bubble baths, soaps and lotions. The health visitor can advise you.

TEMPERATURE is to be regarded as a guide, not a god! There are great variations in what is even a normal temperature – anything between 36°C and 37.5°C (97°F–99°F) may be 'normal'; and where one child may cope with 38.5°C (101°F) without any trouble, another may be very poorly at 37.5°C (99°F). It is, however, generally accepted that a 'high temperature' or 'fever' of more than 38°C (100°F), when measured under the armpit, does not do any child good and should be reduced as soon as possible. Babies under six months old require attention from the doctor immediately if the temperature rises above 39°C (102°F).

Try to reduce the temperature by physically cooling the child: gently sponge her with tepid water and leave it to evaporate; open windows, remove bedclothes, and even introduce a fan if necessary. Paracetamol medicine may be recommended by your doctor; policy varies between practices so it is a good idea to find out what your doctor thinks you should do before it becomes necessary.

A 'low temperature' may follow from, for example, a bout of severe vomiting. Wrap the child up warmly, and cuddle her under the covers with you so that the warmth will gently restore her temperature to normal. Hot-water bottles are not a good idea.

TUMMY ACHE covers a multitude of possibilities. If a young baby pulls his knees up to his chest, it may simply be wind – a thorough 'burping' may cure the problem. In a young child you will know whether it could be constipation; if not that, but there is abdominal pain, it could be a urinary infection, appendicitis, gastroenteritis, or even a strangulated inguinal hernia. See the doctor, especially if there has been persistent vomiting, diarrhoea or a high temperature, and give the baby only sips of water until medical advice has been obtained, or the child feels better.

VOMITING is the forcible ejection of the stomach's contents, not to be confused with the regurgitation of the feed, which many babies do as a matter of course and which is harmless, if a bit messy.

You should call a doctor if a young baby vomits after every feed (occasionally this may be due to pyloric stenosis, a fairly rare conditon which may be rectified by a straightforward operation to enlarge the tube between the intestines and the stomach), or if he loses every feed within a six-hour period.

If vomiting follows violent coughing, whooping cough may need to be considered – see the doctor. For all vomiting, discontinue milk or solid feeds and give sips of water only.

GASTROENTERITIS is an infection of the digestive tract, leading to sickness and diarrhoea. Call the doctor for diagnosis and advice. Dehydration is the major potential problem.

TRAVEL SICKNESS is distressing, especially to those surrounding the victim. Many young children seem to suffer from it, although it is not so common in babies up to about one year. The balance mechanism in the inner ear is upset by the motion of the car/bus/plane/ship. The doctor may suggest a sedative medicine, or you may try to travel when the child will be asleep (assuming he or she co-operates and stays asleep!) Toys and games may prove a sufficient distraction, although some parents think that looking down in the car is a problem. Looking out of windows, for slightly older children, can sometimes be helpful too. Sucking a fruit drop or barley sugar sweet can be comforting – this, again, applies to older children.

EARS are a problem – trouble may be difficult to diagnose at home, and an ear infection left untreated could cause real difficulties later. If there's an otherwise unaccounted for high temperature and general grouchiness, or if the baby or young child is touching his ear or rolling his head, get the ears checked.

Some children have hearing difficulties, and infants are all tested routinely for this at child welfare clinics. If you have reason to suspect some hearing loss, get advice – the earlier that problems are diagnosed, the better chance there is for help to be fully effective. Sometimes it may be behavioural problem which lead to the discovery of hearing loss – a 'difficult child' simply may not have heard clearly.

EYES have an immediate impact on everyone, from Grandma, who wants to know what colour the newborn's eyes are, onwards. It is disconcerting if one eye looks up the chimney while the other looks out of the window, but problems of this sort can be treated very successfully. Babies' eyes may squint when they have wind, but other squinting or wandering of the eyes should be reported to the doctor. Eyes are tested routinely at developmental checks but if you have cause for concern or, for example, a history of astigmatism in the family, ask your doctor for referral to an optician.

If a 'foreign body' gets in the eye, the eye will water and this will usually wash it out. Tears will also help. Don't poke with a handkerchief – this could do more harm than good. If the eyeball gets scratched, seek medical advice.

CONJUNCTIVITIS, or pink eye, is a highly contagious condition – see the doctor.

TEETHING may cause discomfort through infancy, and may begin when your child is very young. There are gels and liquids available to rub on uncomfortable gums, and paracetamol medicine may be given to reduce temperature or pain if necessary. Biting and chewing on hard foods such as apples and raw carrots should be encouraged even before the first tooth emerges. Dribbling usually accompanies these first teeth, and this may be quite prolific. The health visitor can advise on any problems, but be careful not to write all symptoms off as 'teething' as it may be a more serious problem.

The milk teeth are important. If the foundations of good dental health are laid when the child is very young, life will be much easier later. (See page 176.)

COT DEATH is a still unexplained but much-researched phenomenon. An apparently healthy baby simply dies, not always in the cot or in the pram, but sometimes even whilst being held. It is clear that the parents are not responsible in any way for their baby's death: it is not the result of neglect or ill treatment. There are several possible explanations and plenty of literature on the subject.

CRADLE CAP affects babies and pre-school children; it shows up on most baldish babies as brown, crusty patches on the scalp, but older children have it too on the hairline. If it offends, simply rub it with Vaseline or baby oil and gently wash it away.

CROUP is a very distressing condition of the young child. It is a form of laryngitis which so affects the larynx that air can't get through very easily. It usually happens at night: severe coughing is followed by an attempt to cry, which causes a barking sound as the child tries to draw breath to yell. Breathing is very laboured and the child naturally tends to become frightened.

Call the doctor, who may advise that the child should breathe in cold fresh air for a few minutes and then inhale steam; this helps to clear the passages.

ENCEPHALITIS is the inflammation of the brain itself; it follows a similar pattern to meningitis (see below) in terms of cause, diagnosis and treatment.

IMMUNIZATION has become the subject of much debate, especially with regard to whooping cough and measles vaccines. Some experts consider that there is slight risk attached to immunization. Recent developments have provided a second, precautionary shot for the few children at risk of reaction to the measles jab. If you have doubts discuss them fully with your doctor or health visitor before deciding not to have an immunization that could protect your child.

MENINGITIS is a serious complication which may follow fairly straightforward childhood illnesses and which can be successfully treated, especially if detected early. It is the inflammation of the membranes surrounding the brain and is diagnosed by lumbar puncture, usually in hospital. Warning signs are stubborn high temperature, continuous vomiting, abdominal pain, headache or inability to endure light.

WHOOPING COUGH is a very unpleasant illness against which most children can be immunized. The cough is so persistent that the child does not have time to draw breath properly between bouts of coughing, so he forces air through the larynx before it is ready, thus making the whooping sound. The coughing may lead to vomiting. The doctor should see the child at once if you suspect whooping cough. Antibiotics can help, especially if given early.

INDEX

WORKING MOTHER

A PRACTICAL HANDBOOK

Written *by* working mothers *for* working mothers

MARIANNE VELMANS
AND SARAH LITVINOFF

*'Everything you really need to know from pregnancy to your
children's school years'*

It *is* possible to combine motherhood and work successfully, so
that you, your family and your career thrive.

This is the first comprehensive guide to offer advice from the real
experts: other working mothers. Scores of women from all over
Britain have contributed solutions, tips and personal experiences
to back up the facts in this down-to-earth, practical handbook that
leads you right from pregnancy through your children's school
years.

· pregnant at work
  your rights
  your health
  how to dress

· babyhood
  maternity-leave blues
  breastfeeding and work

· under-fives childcare
  nanny
  childminder
  nursery
  other options

· school age
  out-of-school solutions

· your career options

· combatting guilt

· streamlining housework

· your partner

· single mothers

· dealing with crises

NON FICTION AVAILABLE FROM PATHWAY

The prices shown below were correct at the time of going to press. However Transworld Publishers reserve the right to show new prices on covers which may differ from those previously advertised in the text or elsewhere.

13142 3	A Change For The Better	Christine Brady	£3.95
99269 0	Stress Management: A Comprehensive Guide To Wellbeing	Edward Charlesworth & Ronald Nathan	£4.95
13100 8	Guide to Alternative Medicine	Vernon Coleman	£3.95
12757 4	Towards Happy Motherhood: Understanding Post Natal Depression	Maggie Comport	£4.95
17356 1	Running Without Fear	Kenneth Cooper MD	£3.95
17355 3	Fit For Life	Harvey & Marilyn Diamond	£3.50
17491 6	A New Way of Eating	Marilyn Diamond	£2.95
17353 7	The Rotation Diet	Martin Katahn	£3.99
17362 6	Recipes For Allergics	Billie Little	£3.95
17274 3	Recipes for Diabetics	Billie Little & Penny Thorup	£3.95
17273 5	The Herb Book	Ed: John Lust	£4.95
17471 1	The Rice Diet Report	Judy Moscovitz	£3.95
17400 2	How To Make Love To The Same Person For The Rest Of Your Life	Dagmar O'Connor	£3.99
99244 5	Homeopathic Medicine at Home	M. Panos & J. Heimlich	£4.95
12822 8	New Ways to Lower Your Blood Pressure	Claire Safran	£3.95
17272 7	Getting Well Again	Carl & Stephanie Simonton	£3.95
17399 5	Healing Family	Carl Simonton	£4.95
99255 0	Working Mother, A Practical Handbook	Marianne Velmans and Sarah Litvinoff	£5.95
99263 1	Learning To Live With Diabetes	Dr. R M Youngston	£3.50

ORDER FORM

All Corgi/Bantam Books are available at your bookshop or newsagent, or can be ordered direct from the following address:

Corgi/Bantam Books,
Cash Sales Department,
P.O. Box 11, Falmouth, Cornwall TR10 9EN.

Please send a cheque or postal order (no currency) and allow 60p for postage and packing for the first book plus 25p for the second book and 15p for each additional book ordered up to a maximum charge of £1.90 in UK.

B.F.P.O. customers please allow 60p for the first book, 25p for the second book plus 15p per copy for the next 7 books, thereafter 9p per book.

Overseas customers, including Eire, please allow £1.25 for postage and packing for the first book, 75p for the second book, and 28p for each subsequent title ordered.